PUFFIN BOOKS

AFTER MIDNIGHT: A HISTORY OF INDEPENDENT INDIA

Meghaa Gupta's exploits in history are the outcome of an irrepressible urge to contextualise the challenges of the present with the past and make greater sense of the times we live in. She works in children's publishing and firmly believes that all change begins with getting children to read books that demystify the world and its infinite possibilities. Meghaa has contributed to *On this Day: A History of the World in 366 Days* (Dorling Kindersley, 2021) and is the author of the widely-acclaimed *Unearthed: An Environmental History of Independent India* (Puffin, 2020). She curates the children and youth section of the online magazine *sustainabilitynext.in* and is a co-founder at the Green Literature Festival.

ADVANCE PRAISE FOR THE BOOK

I found Meghaa's book objective and devoid of jingoism, something that readers of all ages would benefit from reading, despite her strongly held Indian identity and her lived experience as a woman from privilege. To cover key landmark events in one book is a tough task especially given there are so many milestones in what is now the world's second most populous country. Meghaa delivers despite the challenging job at hand. She examines India's flaws just as critically as its successes, giving credit where it is due but also reflecting upon its hard realities.

—**Disha Shetty**, Journalist, RAF Fellow to the UN, 2019

Meghaa Gupta takes her readers on a whistle-stop tour through the pages of India's history that is illuminating and incisive in equal measure. Drawing its readers in from the very first page, *After Midnight* is sure to enchant young readers with a fantastic gateway to Indian history.

—**Tripurdaman Singh**, Historian and Author of
Sixteen Stormy Days: The Story of the First Amendment to the Constitution of India

AFTER MIDNIGHT

A HISTORY OF INDEPENDENT INDIA

MEGHAA GUPTA

ILLUSTRATIONS BY SAYAN MUKHERJEE

PUFFIN BOOKS

An imprint of Penguin Random House

PUFFIN BOOKS

USA | Canada | UK | Ireland | Australia
New Zealand | India | South Africa | China

Puffin Books is part of the Penguin Random House group of companies whose addresses can be found at global.penguinrandomhouse.com

Published by Penguin Random House India Pvt. Ltd
4th Floor, Capital Tower 1, MG Road,
Gurugram 122 002, Haryana, India

First published in Puffin Books by Penguin Random House India 2022

10 9 8 7 6 5 4 3 2 1

ISBN 9780143458760

Book design and layout by Samar Bansal
Typeset in Charter BT Pro by Manipal Technologies Limited, Manipal
Printed at Thomson Press India Ltd, New Delhi

www.penguin.co.in

MIX
Paper
FSC FSC® C010615

To India and its people . . .

My nationalism, fierce though it is, is not exclusive, is not devised to harm any nation or individual

—Mahatma Gandhi

Contents

PART 3: TRYING TIMES

PART 4: TOWARDS A NEW INDIA

Foreword

Imagine a world without the internet. One where there is no Google, smartphones don't exist, and where most people haven't even heard of electricity. It is a world with barely any cars, very bad roads, and a time when news takes days, if not weeks, to travel. Millions of people live in this world, but most of them can't read or write. They are also very different from each other—of different complexions, food habits, regions, religions, languages, and castes. And yet they are also united: by a civilizational history, and—as some of their leaders tell them—by destiny.

When India was born as a nation-state in 1947, many across the world thought it an experiment doomed to failure. In fact, there were statesmen of great experience and standing *within* India who too believed the country would not last: it had been kept in one piece by British control, and with the departure of that imperial power, bloodshed and civil war would follow. A great amount of blood did flow—in Partition, rioting and more sporadic outbursts of violence—but the nation survived. In a sense, India's endurance made it a wonder of the twentieth century.

But the journey was not easy to begin with, and every milestone of achievement—in science and technology, in military prowess, art, cinema—was also accompanied by many troubling patterns. There was religious animosity, corruption, insurgencies and much else, battles that have not yet been settled. And yet, on the whole, there has been faith in our destiny: India will endure and eventually triumph over its problems. We are still living through that journey. Our time too has its moments of greatness, and seasons of tragedy. And yet we too keep faith.

To write a history of India since Independence is not an easy task. How does one tell the story of a nation? Does one only speak of its achievements, to generate pride among its young? Or does one inform them also of how life is more complicated, exposing them to a healthy dose of sobriety and pragmatism? Meghaa Gupta seeks to strike a balance in *After Midnight*. This book is neither unvarnished pride, nor cynical criticism: it is, instead, an effort in telling India's story with honesty and maturity. You will enjoy reading this book, but it will also make you think; it will give you answers while also leaving you, like any good book, with questions.

For example, you might find it striking that in India's first elections, many women would not even give their names to the government—they preferred to be known as wives and mothers of their men. And yet, in the same country, we have since then had a powerful woman Prime Minister, a woman as President, women as heads of political parties and major companies, and at the helm of our space projects. As Meghaa shows us in chapter after chapter, these ironies exist in every aspect of India's story. They are what make India so distinct, so fascinating and at times even difficult to explain.

To best grasp the book, you must read it with an open mind. You'll read about wars won, and battles lost. It will tell you about the politics of nuclear technology as much as it will about communalism. You will learn about refugees, just as you will of rockets. After all, in a country as large, diverse and complex as India, the story can never be simple. But when you finish reading the book, you'll have learned many new things; and of things you already know, you'd probably think somewhat differently.

When India became free in 1947, our founding fathers and mothers decided that our diversity and internal differences need not be viewed as a problem; instead, by celebrating that diversity, they transformed it into our strength. That ultimately is the message Meghaa leaves us with: that we may all be different, each one of us, but even so we are little rivulets flowing into the same great ocean. That ocean is called India, and it is yours as much as mine: to love, share, protect, defend and ultimately to understand and comprehend.

Manu S. Pillai
Historian and author

Introduction

When I began writing this book, I asked myself, 'What do I like most about my country and being an Indian?' The answer was easy enough—endless diversity. Over the past three and a half decades of my life, I've travelled extensively across India and lived in three of its four major metros—Delhi, Mumbai and Chennai. Everywhere I went, I found people who were different from me. They looked different. They spoke a different language at home. They followed a different religion. They ate different food . . . Initially, I felt a little lost and missed the comfort of familiarity.

Differences may seem daunting when you first encounter them. But they can also be deeply enriching. India's diversity has allowed me to make room for many different things in my life. I speak English and Hindi at home, but I've also picked up simple words and phrases like 'Hello', 'How are you?' and 'Thank you' in eight other languages. I've learned some of them from watching regional cinema or reading translations of regional literature. The others have been taught to me by domestic helpers, auto drivers, shopkeepers, waiters at restaurants . . . Friends have added a few colourful curse words to this multilingual dictionary! My pronunciation may not always be up to the mark, but every time I meet someone who speaks these languages, I attempt to greet them in their mother tongue. It's a different matter that the results are sometimes hilarious. I've learnt that some words have gone out of fashion. At times, my pronunciation has changed the meaning of a word entirely!

Food is my weakness. Although I'm a vegetarian, this has been a non-issue in India. I've relished dal bati churma in Rajasthan, dal makhani in Punjab, aloo pitika in Assam, puchka in Kolkata, vegetarian biryani in Hyderabad, thepla in Gujarat, vada-pav in Mumbai and sambar-rice in Chennai—and that's barely scraping the surface. I'm a Hindu and I've been to many different temples. But I've also been to mosques, gurudwaras and churches. No one has asked me what religion I follow. I've been treated as any other worshipper. My home in Delhi is decorated with little souvenirs that keep reminding me of my journeys. The places, the people and all the different things I learnt from them.

When India became independent, many people around the world wondered whether this land full of differences would ever be able to remain united as a nation. Indeed, its differences have often become a cause of conflict between people who speak different languages, belong to different ethnic groups or follow different religions. Yet, India has persisted through thick and thin. It has faced communal crises, insurgencies, wars and many such perils arising out of differences, but one way or another, its map continues to remain whole, seventy-five years after Independence.

In 1969, a British journalist Don Taylor wrote, 'When one looks at this vast country . . . it seems incredible that one nation could emerge . . . and yet there is a resilience about India which seems an assurance of survival. There is something which can only be described as an Indian spirit.' *After Midnight* is essentially about this Indian spirit that has overcome great odds to find its place in the world. Learning this history is a reminder of our shared humanity and our ability to rise above all that separates and frustrates us in the pursuit of great endeavours.

Meghaa
10 May 2022

Freedom at Last

Between 1939 and 1945, the world was in the midst of the devastating Second World War. On one side were Germany, Italy and Japan, together known as the Axis powers. Resisting their forces were the United States of America, Britain, the Soviet Union (USSR) and a few other countries, who formed the Allies. Even though the Allies eventually won the war, the road to this victory was covered in countless corpses and most of Europe lay in tatters.

The war had weakened Britain and its hold over the mighty British empire. Spread over large parts of the world, including India, the empire was steadily losing its strength and could no longer exert the same amount of power over its territories as it once had. A majority of its people wanted Britain to focus all its resources on rebuilding itself after the war instead of retaining its supremacy over foreign lands. Of course, not everyone agreed with this, especially not the British leader Winston Churchill, who had led the country during the war. Yet, the will of the people prevailed. Churchill's party lost the elections that followed the war. The new political party that came to power, headed by Clement Attlee, decided to immediately implement the wishes of the people—granting independence to many countries that had been part of the British empire.

Fighting for Freedom

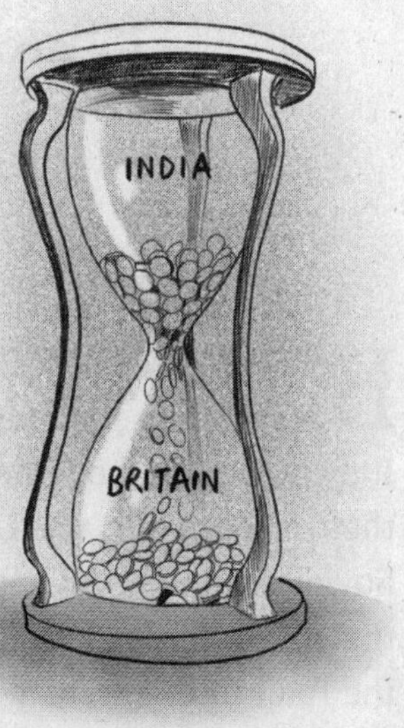

Among the first of these was India—the jewel in the crown of the empire—a land that had once been so wealthy that it lured the British East India Company to trade with it and eventually seize control. In 1857, a large mass of Indians mounted a revolt against the company's control. But it was crushed by the empire's military prowess. In the years following the revolt, British control over India expanded exponentially. The administration became better organized with provinces being directly ruled by the British and princely states ruled by various nawabs and maharajas under British control. By the 1880s, the British were so firmly entrenched in India that they claimed they could rule over it for a thousand years. They did, however, find stiff opposition to their rule, especially in a political party called the Indian National Congress.

The Congress began its resistance by making polite petitions to the British government, demanding self-rule for India. But its demands were largely ignored. By the early 1900s, firebrand leaders like Bal Gangadhar Tilak and Lala Lajpat Rai shunned politeness and began talking assertively of freedom from British rule. Their protests were crushed forcefully.

When Britain was engaged in the First World War between 1914 and 1918, the British government sought out the cooperation of Indians in return for granting them a greater role in the running of their country. But, when the war ended, it went back on its word. Instead, in April 1919, India was shocked by a horrific massacre at Jallianwala Bagh in Amritsar. The British officer Reginald Dyer ordered his soldiers to open fire at hundreds of men, women and children who had gathered to celebrate the festival of Baisakhi. The violence sparked off a nationwide freedom movement. At the helm of this movement was a man named Mohandas Karamchand Gandhi, whose relentless emphasis on non-violence made people call him 'Mahatma' (noble soul). Gandhi's non-violent struggle against British rule played a defining role in India's fight for freedom.

Mahatma Gandhi marching with his followers

Under his guidance, the Congress led three major movements against the British—the Non-Cooperation Movement of 1920, the Civil Disobedience Movement of 1930 and the Quit India Movement of 1942. These movements became a major obstacle for the British government. Controlling the movements used up a lot of the empire's resources and by the end of the Second World War, it found itself lacking the physical force, will and conviction needed to battle this growing opposition and sustain its rule. Eventually, on 15 August 1947, the British left India, and the Congress, under Jawaharlal Nehru, came to lead the country.

Nationhood

Newly Independent India was a land stripped of its riches and wracked by disease and famine. An unwieldy jumble of British provinces and hundreds of princely states, few believed that it could survive as an independent nation, especially when its people spoke so many different languages and belonged to so many different ethnicities. Social inequalities and conflict were omnipresent.

People were divided along age-old barriers of caste—the social groups into which they were born, which historically determined the work they did. There were also massive differences in wealth. Some people rolled in it while many found it hard to manage even two meals a day. Not surprisingly, people belonging to lower castes, who had long been discriminated against and forced into low-paying menial jobs, were poorer than others. Cutting across these divides of caste and class was gender. Regarded as breadwinners, men were almost always considered superior to women and female infanticide (killing newborn baby girls) was very common.

To make matters worse, at the time of Independence, the land was partitioned into Hindu-majority India and Muslim-majority Pakistan. Religious differences drove a deep wedge between the two communities and countries. What unifying idea could such a diverse and divided land possibly take on? How could it best serve the interests of all its people?

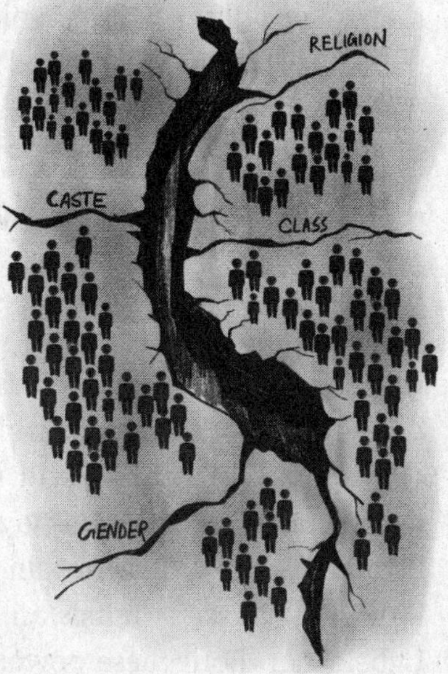

Power to the People

For Independent India, the answer to many of its dilemmas lay in democracy—a government made of representatives elected by the people to work for them. At the heart of democracy lay the right to vote and have a say in the running of the country.

The right to vote had long been considered a privilege to be restricted to those with wealth, influence and education. In many parts of the world, women and people belonging to lower social groups had to fight for voting rights. But Independent India gave all its people above a fixed age the right to vote and determine who would run the country on their behalf. This was considered a truly bold and remarkable step, especially because most of its people were far too poor and could barely read and write. But in choosing to empower them with voting rights, India gave its people, irrespective of their many differences, a voice and opportunity to express their hopes, fears, anger and joy, and determine the fate of their land.

A Nation within the World

Independent India was a deeply divided country born in a deeply divided world. Not too long after the war, the world found itself in the midst of deep tension between the democracies of the West, led by the United States (US), and the communist countries in the East, led by the USSR—a group comprising present-day Armenia, Azerbaijan, Belarus, Estonia, Georgia, Kazakhstan, Kyrgyzstan, Latvia, Lithuania, Moldova, Russia, Tajikistan, Turkmenistan, Ukraine and Uzbekistan. Both these power blocs wanted to establish the supremacy of their ideology, which led to a 'cold war' between them. Democratic countries believed in giving power to the people. They had multiple political parties and people could vote for any of them. People could also form their own political parties and contest elections. However, in communist countries, power usually belonged to a single political party that formed the government and ruled over the people.

Determined to preserve its new-found independence, India refused to align itself with either of the power blocs. It may have opted to be a democracy, but it also extended a hand of friendship towards the communist countries. In 1961, Nehru joined Yugoslavia's Josip Broz Tito, Egypt's Gamal Abdel Nasser, Ghana's Kwame Nkrumah and Indonesia's Sukarno to officially create the Non-Aligned Movement—an international group of countries that refused to be officially aligned with or against any power bloc. Amidst the global tension caused by the Cold War, these leaders saw non-alignment as a way of safeguarding national independence, sovereignty, territory and security, and doing what was best for their people without worrying about which power bloc they belonged to.

Beating the Odds

The fate of democratic India has been questioned repeatedly since Independence. Many people have predicted its downfall time and again. After all, how can democracy function effectively in a country so diverse and divided? Eventually, some power had to prevail. It was easy to think that sooner or later, India would fall into the hands of a powerful dictator who would rule over its people with an iron fist, eroding the country's hard-won independence. Yet, with every election and change in government, India has squashed such beliefs. In Jawaharlal Nehru and Indira Gandhi, it has had some of the longest serving, democratically elected prime ministers. During the 1970s, it even witnessed a period of twenty-one months when democracy was suspended.

Yet, the history of Independent India is a story of how the world's largest democracy has continued to survive. Of how a nation has overcome grave challenges to carve its own unique identity. In many ways, this is one of the greatest underdog-beating-the-odds stories in the world—full of blood, sweat, tragedy and triumph.

PART 1

LAYING THE FOUNDATIONS

1

A Divided Land, a Broken Home

Midnight was an hour away. The assembly hall of the Council House (Parliament House) in Delhi was brilliantly lit and decorated with India's new national flag. After a long and hard struggle, the country was finally going to win freedom from British rule. However, astrologers had predicted that 15 August 1947 was an inauspicious day. So the celebration had started before midnight on the 14th.

The ceremony began with the singing of the patriotic song 'Vande Mataram', followed by a two-minute silence in the memory of those who had lost their lives in the freedom struggle. Several speeches were given, but the one that went down in history was made by Jawaharlal Nehru, the first Prime Minister of free India:

At the stroke of the midnight hour, when the world sleeps, India will awake to life and freedom . . .

Jawaharlal Nehru

Outside the Council House, thousands waited with bated breath, listening to the speech through loudspeakers. After months of horrible heat, monsoon had finally arrived. Suddenly, there was a sound of thunder and it began to rain. The moment the clock struck twelve, a spontaneous cheer went up. A conch was blown and the sound echoed through the hall. The crowds danced and sang on the streets. Lights glowed everywhere. India was finally a free nation. People shouted, '*Mahatma Gandhi ki Jai!*' in honour of the man who had led their non-violent freedom struggle. But where was Mahatma Gandhi?

The Mahatma's Misery

Away from all the pomp, a mournful Mahatma Gandhi was fasting and praying in a ramshackle building in Calcutta (now Kolkata). Freedom had come at a terrible cost. British India was going to be partitioned to create Pakistan–a separate country for Muslims. Communal violence had claimed thousands of lives. Gandhi, who had always followed the path of non-violence, could not bear to see the bloodshed.

How had such a tragedy come to pass? Why had Hindus and Muslims who spent a large part of the freedom struggle fighting together suddenly become enemies? But there was

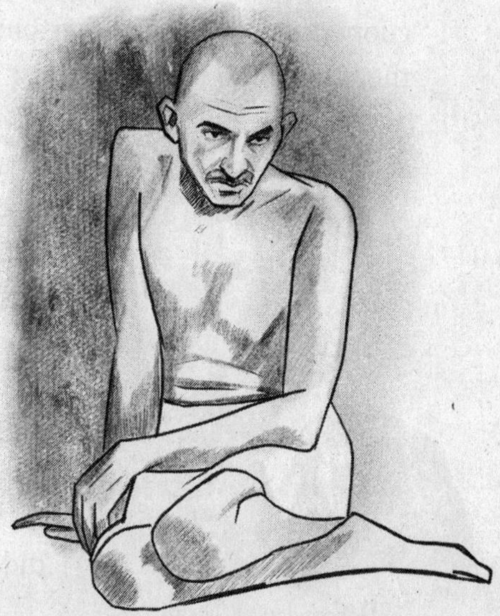

Mahatma Gandhi

nothing sudden about the animosity. It had been brewing for a long time . . . aided by members of both the communities and the British.

The Roots of Discord

In 1857, Indians of all communities, including Hindus and Muslims, had fought together to drive out the British. Even though the revolt was eventually crushed, it made the British realize that a united India could pose a threat to their rule. So they began to play upon the differences between the people and divide them along communal lines.

In 1885, a group of educated, middle-class Indians had formed the Indian National Congress that envisioned a modern India where all communities, castes and religions were equal. However, encouraged by the British divide-and-rule policy, a small group of Muslims formed a separate political party called the Muslim League in 1906, which was dedicated to the cause of Muslims. Initially, the Congress and the League cooperated with each other, but by the 1930s tensions between them began to rise rapidly.

Mohammad Ali Jinnah

In 1937, when Indians were finally allowed to contest elections in British provinces, the Congress won enough seats to form governments in several provinces. But the League, headed by Mohammad Ali Jinnah, fared poorly and its offer to form governments together with the Congress was ignored. Having won by such a wide margin, the Congress did not feel the need to include members of the League in its governments. This turned the League against the Congress and it cemented the idea of a separate nation for Muslims, claiming that Muslims would be overpowered by the Hindu majority in India. This campaign was hugely successful. In the elections held in 1946, Muslim voters almost unanimously voted for the League and the Congress lost a majority of the seats reserved for Muslims in the provincial governments.

With the Muslim vote firmly behind it, the League began to insist on Partition. On 16 August 1946, it called for a nationwide protest by Muslims for the creation of Pakistan. Hindu–Muslim riots broke out in Calcutta and soon spread to other parts of the country. Old differences, anger and resentment came to the surface as people robbed and killed each other. The scale of horrific communal violence made the idea of Partition inevitable, even to those who opposed it vehemently.

Communal riots broke out in August 1946, when the Muslim League called for a nationwide protest for the creation of Pakistan

Events Move Fast

In February 1947, British Prime Minister Clement Attlee announced that the British would leave India by June 1948. The next month a new viceroy (head of the British administration in India), Lord Mountbatten, arrived and began to discuss the terms of British withdrawal.

The atmosphere was tense. Communal discord ran deep. The League refused to budge from its demand for a new nation and most Congress leaders realized that there was no other way around this problem. On 3 June 1947, Mountbatten announced the plan to partition British India over All-India Radio. The very next day, he informed the Indian leadership that the British would leave India in August 1947 instead of June 1948. An empire that had been built over two centuries was going to pull out in a mere ten weeks! The viceroy believed that once the plan for Partition was announced, communal violence would rage free and delays in the British departure would only make things worse.

In July, with a little over a month left for Independence, a British lawyer Cyril Radcliffe was summoned to divide the land. He had to draw borders across the British-era provinces of Punjab and Bengal in a way that would leave a majority of Hindus and Sikhs in India and Muslims in the new nation of Pakistan.

Dividing a Land

Both Punjab and Bengal had a Muslim majority, but they also had lakhs of Hindus. Bengal had a long history of communal conflict between Hindus and Muslims. A large part of its Hindu population had accepted the idea of Partition. By contrast, the Hindu community of Punjab was unwilling to accept it and hoped, till the very end, that Partition would be avoided. The most telling difference between the two provinces was the presence of Sikhs in Punjab. Partition would mean that their holy city Amritsar, in east Punjab, would remain in India, while Nankana Saheb, the birthplace of Guru Nanak—the founder of their religion—that lay in west Punjab, would go to Pakistan. They were against parting with either.

Anticipating trouble, Evan Jenkins, the governor of undivided Punjab wrote to Mountbatten, saying that no community in the province would accept Partition. While the Muslims had hoped to get the entire province, the Hindus and Sikhs were fearful of losing Lahore, which lay in the west. But there was no going back on the decision to partition Punjab. So, on 1 August 1947, a Punjab Boundary Force was set up to control any violence that broke out. Jenkins asked Mountbatten for more troops but these were not available.

On 15 August India celebrated Independence with much fanfare. Gandhi's mood lifted when he heard of large crowds of both communities rejoicing together. He held a prayer meeting in Calcutta, urging the communities to fight off the 'communal virus' and drink the sweet 'nectar of friendliness'.

Pakistan had celebrated its Independence Day on 14 August. When Radcliffe's border was announced in Bengal, the situation remained largely peaceful even though its eastern wing had gone to Pakistan. But an explosion was about to occur across the country.

A Bloody Carnage

Rioting began almost as soon as Radcliffe's border in Punjab was announced on 17 August. The Punjab Boundary Force proved to be ineffective against the rioters. Hindus and Sikhs fell upon the Muslims in east Punjab, which had been retained by India, while Muslims were killing Hindus and Sikhs in west Punjab, which had gone to Pakistan. In the midst of this violence, there began a mass exodus, with Muslims fleeing Hindu-majority India, and Hindus and Sikhs fleeing Muslim-majority Pakistan. Nowhere in known history had so many people been displaced in a matter of days. A madness seized the mobs and countless men, women and children were butchered in scenes of unimaginable cruelty. Tensions began to flare up in Bengal too. Gandhi was heartbroken.

On 1 September 1947, fifty people were killed in communal clashes in Calcutta. Gandhi went on a fast and the very next day, rioters laid down their arms. Scenes of communal harmony took place in different parts of the city and leaders from the Congress, the League and other parties reassured Gandhi that there would be no further rioting. He finally broke his fast, and a few days later, made his way to Delhi.

The Muslims in Delhi were frightened. Their lives, homes and places of worship were under attack. Gandhi put his impending visit to Punjab on hold, and visited refugee camps and hospitals, pleading with Hindus, Sikhs and Muslims to maintain peace. He urged the Congress to pass a resolution to protect the rights of minority communities. But the situation was not conducive to peace.

Hindu and Sikh refugees, who had to leave behind their lives in Pakistan and had suffered deeply in the carnage, were not as willing to forgive and forget. Their grief was not lost on the Hindus and Sikhs in India. Attacks on Muslims continued and on 13 January 1948, Gandhi went on a fast again. He appealed to the Hindus and Muslims in India to live in peace and brotherhood. He appealed to the government in Pakistan to stop driving out the Hindu and Sikh minorities and control the violence against them. Finally, he appealed to the Government of India to release the share of money owed to the Government of Pakistan in the aftermath of Partition.

The Partition was not merely a division of land and people. From armed forces, money, ration, roads and railways to pens, paper, tables, chairs, books, cars, typewriters, lathis, guns . . . it also involved a massive division of administrative resources.

The Light Is Gone

Gandhi's health was declining. Yet, he refused to break his fast. On 15 January 1948, the Government of India decided to release the funds owed to the Government of Pakistan. Assurances of peace were made by the rioters. A Central Peace Committee was formed on 17 January with representatives from different parties. A day later it pledged to 'protect the life, property and faith of Muslims' and prevent the violence that had played out in Delhi from happening again. Finally, Gandhi broke his fast.

On 20 January 1948, an angry Punjabi refugee hurled a bomb at a prayer meeting led by Gandhi. However, it exploded at some distance and no one was hurt. Gandhi was undaunted and continued his prayer meetings. On the evening of 30 January 1948, as he made his way to his prayer meeting, a young man came forward, as if to greet him. When Gandhi raised his hands to respond with a namaste, the man, Nathuram Godse, took out a gun and fired three shots. Gandhi murmured the name of God and fell to the ground. A Hindu, Godse was angry with Gandhi because he felt that Gandhi had been pandering to the Muslims. The Father of the Nation, whom many called 'the greatest figure of the twentieth century' had died speaking up for communal harmony and equality. India was inconsolable. The enormity of his loss stalled the bloodshed.

India was independent but it had been divided along tense communal lines. Gandhi was dead. The British had finally left, but in their wake was an underdeveloped country with a severe food shortage and crores of poor and uneducated people. What would happen to this land? Would it ever find peace and prosperity? The story of Independent India had barely begun, yet, pessimists around the world were already writing its end.

2

The Refugee Crisis

People often leave their homes to go to other countries across the world. Sometimes they leave willingly, for example, in search of better opportunities. However, many are also forced to migrate because their home countries become unsafe for them. This can happen due to many reasons such as war or because they are threatened on the grounds of their race, religion, membership of a particular social group or political opinions. Such migrants are called refugees. If the country to which they go does not legally recognize them, they become 'illegal immigrants'.

One of the most urgent crises facing newly independent India was the massive wave of refugees who poured into its territory in the wake of the Partition (*see page 6*). The problem was especially intense in the north-west, where Hindus and Sikhs from Muslim-majority West Pakistan were arriving in droves in the midst of unimaginable communal violence on both sides of the border.

>1,00,00,000

The number of people displaced by Partition

Hundreds of refugee camps had been set up in various places in Punjab, Rajasthan and Delhi to house the refugees, but they proved to be inadequate. One of the largest camps at Kurukshetra, in erstwhile Punjab, which had been planned to accommodate 1,00,000 refugees, eventually came to shelter about three times that number! It resembled a city of tents that kept growing, as more and more refugees flocked in—sometimes as many as 20,000 a day.

Refugee camps often resembled an ever-growing city of tents

Refugees from West Pakistan spilled over on the streets in cities, occupying every conceivable place, from pavements and railway stations to gardens, schools, colleges, old monuments. Apart from Delhi, many refugees, especially those from Sindh (Sindhis), also went to Bombay (now Mumbai), Poona (now Pune) and Ahmedabad. Resettling this growing population—providing them permanent homes and livelihoods—was an enormous challenge for India. In 1950, the Ministry of Relief and Rehabilitation was set up to attend to the various needs of refugees.

A bulk of the refugees in the north-west were farmers and they were resettled on land in Punjab that had been vacated by those who had fled to West Pakistan. They were allotted medium-sized holdings and given loans to procure seeds and equipment for farming. For most of them, what they got hardly compared to what they had left behind. Yet, they plodded on, digging wells, building new houses and planting crops. Soon, the deserted lands of Punjab were humming with new life.

Those who were not farmers were allotted land in cities. The government also began building new industrial townships such as Faridabad, located on the outskirts of Delhi, to accommodate them. Homes were built, power-plants and factories were set up and skill-development initiatives helped the newly settled residents find work in factories and set up shops and small production units.

Many well-known colonies in Delhi, such as Lajpat Nagar, Rajendra Nagar and Patel Nagar, were originally built by refugees on land allotted to them by the government.

Bit by bit, aided by their own thrift and inventiveness, the refugees made the best of what was given to them and built new lives in India. By the 1950s, India was beginning to get a grip on the refugee-crises in the north-west. But things were beginning to get worse in the east.

Raj Sethi was only a baby when her family left West Pakistan to come to India. 'My father was thriving in his job at a factory in Rawalpindi. Fearing trouble, he brought us to India three months before the Partition. But it was meant to be a temporary move. He had never intended to settle here.' Every time she remembers her father, she tears up. 'He could never reconcile himself to the fact that we would not be able to return to Pakistan. His anger and resentment against fate took away all our joy. The life he had worked so hard to build there was lost forever.'

Complications in the East

In Punjab, the post-Partition exodus had happened in one big rush over the course of a year. In newly carved out Bengal, however, it was spread out over many years and happened in successive waves.

People were prepared for the division. The Hindus and Muslims of Bengal shared a cultural affinity. They spoke the same language and ate the same food. So, the hope was that the two communities could live in peace despite the Partition. But growing incidents of communal violence in Muslim-majority East Pakistan began to drive hordes of Hindus across the border. This complicated resettlement, because there were hardly any vacant plots to make room for these refugees. Moreover, the resettlement process in the east was far less organized, as the government had not expected trouble and taken proactive measures to settle refugees. Despite this, the migration continued, and things became worse because of events in East Pakistan in 1971.

Creation of Bangladesh

The Partition had separated the two halves of Pakistan—one in the east and the other in the west—by thousands of kilometres of Indian territory. East Pakistan felt neglected by the Pakistani leadership based in the west. Resources were not distributed fairly and the east was poorer than the west in most ways. Even culturally, the two halves of Pakistan were very different from each other, with most of the population speaking Bengali in the east and Urdu in the west. So, when Urdu was declared the national language of the new nation, many in the east became resentful. This tension and discontentment reached its boiling point after Pakistan's first election in 1970.

The Awami League, headed by the Bengali-Muslim leader Sheikh Mujibur Rahman, swept to power by winning an absolute majority of 160 seats, all of which were in East Pakistan. However, General Yahya Khan, who was the President of Pakistan at the time, refused to allow this. He imposed martial law in the east, imprisoned Rahman and appointed General Tikka Khan as the leader of East Pakistan. Thereafter, the army began a systematic crackdown, code-named Operation Searchlight, on the Bengali population. Lakhs of Bengalis were killed, regardless of their religion. This led to a mass exodus into India. The Indian government offered refuge to the people streaming in, at refugee camps along the border in West Bengal, Assam, Tripura and Meghalaya.

The Mukti Bahini—a guerrilla force of Bengalis from East Pakistan who were resisting its military—also took refuge in India. It comprised officers and soldiers who had defected from East Pakistan's army as well as independent volunteers. They conducted training camps and began launching attacks against the forces occupying their homeland. Even though India hosted them, its military did not get involved in the hostility between East and West Pakistan.

1,00,00,000

The approximate number of refugees who arrived in India from East Pakistan in 1971.

In December 1971, West Pakistan attacked India and a full-fledged war broke out. Indian forces launched massive air strikes alongside on-ground action. For the first time, even the navy was deployed to fend off the attackers. India also began to move its troops and tanks into East Pakistan. With the help of the Mukti Bahini as well as local civilians, it made swift progress and took control of East Pakistan in a little less than two weeks. On 16 December 1971, General Niazi—the Pakistani commander in the East—surrendered, and the next day, a ceasefire was declared. East Pakistan became the new nation of Bangladesh, headed by Rahman. It was a tremendous victory for India that helped to resolve, to some extent, the dire refugee crisis in East India. Freed from the threat of persecution, many Bengali refugees returned to Bangladesh. However, many also chose to remain in India and the migrations did not stop.

Mujibur Rahman (L) and army generals (R) signing the Instrument of Surrender that ended the war and recognised the creation of the new nation of Bangladesh

A POROUS BORDER

The border between India and Bangladesh is among the most complex borders anywhere in the world. It is over 4000 km long and close to 30 per cent of it runs through waterbodies and the Sundarban mangroves. The river Brahmaputra, which flows through this border, is often turbulent and keeps eating away its banks. As such, the boundary between land and water keeps changing and is hard to monitor.

Tensions in the North-east

In the years since Partition, the north-east has become an entry point for the largest number of migrants in Independent India and has ended up housing a majority of them. This has angered local communities, who claim that the large population of migrants has made them minorities in their own land, taking away their resources and opportunities. The tension around migration has led to a lot of trouble in many north-eastern states, especially Assam.

The state of Assam shares its borders with West Bengal, several states in the north-east as well as the countries of Bangladesh and Bhutan. Although Assamese is the state language, Bengali is also widely spoken. Unfortunately, the Assamese have long felt dominated by the Bengalis. During the colonial era, Bengalis occupied important positions in the British administration, allowing them to exercise greater power over the Assamese. The British also brought in a large population of Bengali peasants to cultivate the land. This wave of Bengali migrants continued even after Independence and became especially intense in the 1970s when India went to war against East Pakistan, leading to the creation of Bangladesh. During this decade, the number of registered voters in Assam increased from 62 lakhs to nearly 90 lakhs, primarily on account of migrants from Bangladesh.

Frustrated by the continuous migration and the threat of being dominated by Bengalis, a powerful group of Assamese students called the All Assam Students' Union began a popular agitation, known as the Assam Movement, in 1979. As years went by, this movement became increasingly violent. On 15 August 1985, the Assam Accord was signed between the government and the leaders of the Assam Movement to reduce the number of migrants in the state. The government also amended the Citizenship Act of 1955 to make room for the provisions of the Accord.

ASSAM ACCORD

The Assam Accord marked out three important dates that determined the fate of migrants.

Before 1 January 1966: *Migrants who came in this period would be considered citizens and granted voting rights.*

From 1 January 1966–24 March 1971: *Migrants who came in during this period would be allowed to stay, provided they registered themselves as foreigners. This population would be denied voting rights for the next 10 years.*

On or after 25 March 1971: *Migrants who came in this period would be detected and deported.*

NRC and CAA

Owing to tensions over migration, India had started a National Register of Citizens (NRC) for Assam as early as 1951. It sought to identify and register Indian citizens in the state. However, this register was not maintained and neither was it mentioned in the Assam Accord. In 2005, the government began a discussion on updating the NRC to fulfil the promises made in the Assam Accord. A few years later, in 2009, an NGO called Assam Public Works moved the Supreme Court, pleading for names of undocumented migrants to be removed from the voters' list. They wanted the NRC updation process to begin. Their petition came up for hearing in August 2013 and in December the Supreme Court directed the government to begin the process of updating the NRC. This exercise finally began in 2015. The first list of illegal immigrants that was released in 2017 had 35 lakh people. This number dropped to around 19 lakhs in the final revised list released in 2019.

The same year, the government again amended the Citizenship Act, allowing all those who had entered India up to 31 December 2014 to apply for citizenship. Furthermore, while the original act stated that a person should have resided in India for at least eleven years in order to be eligible for citizenship, the amended Act reduced this period to five years. But there was one important catch—these amendments only applied to illegal immigrants who were Hindus, Sikhs, Buddhists, Jains, Parsis or Christians from Afghanistan, Bangladesh and Pakistan. Muslims were excluded. The government claimed that this was because the likelihood of Muslims facing religious persecution in these Muslim-majority countries was remote.

The new amendment, called the Citizenship Amendment Act (CAA), led to widespread protests across India. In the north-east, people were angry primarily because the amendment had violated the Assam Accord by extending the cut-off date to apply for citizenship from 25 March 1971 (as stated in the Accord) to 31 December 2014. This meant that more migrants could now end up as legal residents of the north-east and thus obtain voting rights. Predictably, the backlash was severe and violence raged through Assam and other states of the north-east.

In other parts of India people were angry because they felt that together with the NRC, the CAA discriminated between migrants on the basis of religion and this could have larger consequences if the NRC was applied throughout the country. However, supporters of the CAA claimed that it only made an exception for Muslim migrants from Muslim-majority countries and did not discriminate against Muslims who were citizens of India.

The Refugee Saga

Despite all this confusion and violence, India still doesn't have a separate, all-encompassing law or policy that clearly identifies refugees who are eligible to apply for citizenship and distinguishes them from illegal immigrants, irrespective of their country of origin. Instead, it continues to rely on measures like the Assam Accord, CAA and NRC that don't apply to all migrants entering its territory.

Many people attribute this to politics. The large population of refugees makes them a potentially important set of voters for political parties, especially in the north-east. The issue of migration is raised frequently in the run-up to elections. While some parties seek votes by denying legal recognition to refugees, others try and appease them in hopes of winning their vote. That's why granting citizenship and voting rights to refugees remains a contentious issue.

Major Refugee Groups in India

TIBETANS

Many Tibetans escaped to India in 1959, following a revolt against the Chinese forces occupying their land. Most of them reside in Karnataka, Himachal Pradesh, Uttarakhand, Arunachal Pradesh, West Bengal and Ladakh. McLeod Ganj in Himachal Pradesh is home to the Dalai Lama and also houses a Tibetan Government-in-Exile. (*Also see page 72-74*)

ROHINGYAS

Brutal military crackdowns forced lakhs of Rohingyas, a Muslim minority in Myanmar, to escape to neighbouring countries. Many of them entered India in 2011 and afterwards. The Indian government considers them illegal immigrants and wants them to return to Myanmar.

CHAKMAS AND HAJONGS

Tribal groups from the Chittagong Hill Tracts of Bangladesh, the Chakmas are predominantly Buddhists, while the Hajongs are Hindus. During the 1960s, a large population of both these tribes entered India because their lands were drowned by the Kaptai Dam and also because they faced religious persecution in Muslim-majority East Pakistan. Most of them reside in Arunachal Pradesh.

SRI LANKAN TAMILS

Many Tamil people escaped from Sri Lanka when a civil war broke out between the Sri Lankan government and the Liberation Tigers of Tamil Eelam (LTTE), who wanted an independent Tamil state in the Sinhalese-majority country. The war began in the 1980s and ended twenty-six years later, when Sri Lankan armed forces defeated the LTTE. In 2022, an economic crisis in Sri Lanka led to another influx of refugees. Most of them reside in Tamil Nadu.

3

Remaking the Map

The map of British India in 1947, was like a giant puzzle. It had eleven provinces that were directly administered by the British. These were surrounded by over 500 princely states ruled by various nawabs and maharajas under British control. There were also a few small territories controlled by the French and the Portuguese.

Post-Independence, the North-West Frontier Province, areas of Sindh, Balochistan and West Punjab would become West Pakistan, while areas in east Bengal would become East Pakistan. The remaining provinces would be part of India. But a large part of the puzzle—the princely states—remained unsolved. Once the British left, the princely states could either choose to join India or Pakistan, or become independent countries.

Most of the princely states were situated close to Indian territory and India wanted all of them to join it. This was a massive mission, one that needed hard-work, wisdom and foresight. Luckily, India had just the people for the job: Deputy Prime Minister Sardar Vallabhbhai Patel and his secretary V.P. Menon. In June 1947, the States Department was set up, and Patel and Menon began piecing together the puzzle.

Sardar Patel (L) and V.P. Menon (R)

Wooing the Princely States

The princely states were very different from each other. Some were large, while others were tiny. Many large states had their own railway, currency and stamps. Very few states had any form of modern education. Most of the rulers depended on the British for their political and economic might and many did not trust the Congress. When the British announced that they were finally leaving India, some rulers wanted their states to become independent countries.

Patel threw a series of lunch parties to meet the rulers and invited them to join the Congress in framing a new constitution for independent India. He also wrote to the influential dewans (chief ministers) of the princely states, urging them to ask their rulers to come to terms with the Congress. Soon, he won over several important rulers, such as the Gaekwad of Baroda, the Scindia of Gwalior, the Maharaja of Bikaner and the Maharaja of Patiala, who in turn helped to bring other princely states on India's side.

The Congress requested the British government not to support or recognize any fanciful claims of independence being made by the princely states. It also requested the British Viceroy, Lord Mountbatten, to help in wooing the rulers—and he did this most effectively. On 25 July 1947, decked out in all his finery, Mountbatten gave an important speech, telling the princely states that it would be hard for them to survive independently once the British left India.

Between them, Patel, Menon and Mountbatten had worked out two important agreements: an Instrument of Accession for the states to accede to, or join India, and a Standstill Agreement, which meant that the agreements or arrangements that had existed between the British and the individual states would continue, with the Indian government replacing the British until new arrangements were made. Mountbatten began pressing the states to accede. He told them that if they acceded before 15 August 1947, he would help them get decent terms with the Congress. But if they did not listen, they could get into trouble as nationalist anger might turn against them and the British would not come to their rescue.

By Independence Day, barring a bit of drama, virtually all the states had signed the Instrument of Accession. The only states that Patel and Menon had failed to woo were Junagadh, Hyderabad and Kashmir.

Among the princely states, thirteen eventually acceded to Pakistan: Khairpur, Bahawalpur, Chitral, Dir, Swat, Amb, Hunza, Nagar, Gilgit, Las Bela, Kharan, Makran and Kalat. They were primarily Muslim majority areas that bordered West Pakistan.

The Drama Before Accession…

TRAVANCORE

C.P. Ramaswamy Aiyar

Travancore was among the first princely states to resist accession. Located along the coast on the southern tip of India, it had a highly educated population and thriving international trade. Sir C.P. Ramaswamy Aiyar, the influential dewan of Travancore, made it clear that once the British left, Travancore was perfectly capable of being an independent unit. However, in a sensational turn of events, on 25 July 1947 Aiyar was attacked on his way to a musical concert. The attacker knifed his face and body and the dewan had to be rushed for an emergency surgery. The incident shook him up, and from his hospital bed, he advised the maharaja to accede to India.

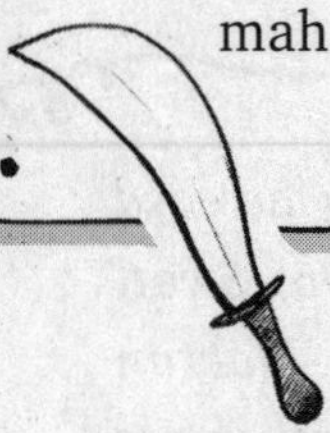

BHOPAL

Hamidullah Khan

The Nawab of Bhopal, Hamidullah Khan, who had been close friends with Mountbatten, was extremely unhappy at the prospect of acceding and losing all his powers. He exchanged several letters with the viceroy, who cajoled him patiently. Following Mountbatten's speech on 25 July, the nawab received reports of a number of accessions by his fellow princes. He finally relented and signed the Instrument of Accession on 14 August, on one condition: no one should be told of his accession till ten days after Independence!

JODHPUR

Hanwant Singh

Jodhpur was an old and large state with a Hindu ruler and a largely Hindu population. Even though the Maharaja of Jodhpur, Hanwant Singh, had indicated his willingness to join India, Mohammad Ali Jinnah began wooing him to join Pakistan. Since Jodhpur also shared a border with Pakistan, the maharaja wondered if he could get better terms from it. However, Patel intervened with his own enticing offer. Meanwhile, nobles and village headmen as well as the ruler of the adjoining state of Jaisalmer questioned the maharaja about how comfortable he would be if he joined a Muslim-majority nation. Eventually, the maharaja came around and agreed to sign the Instrument of Accession. However, he pulled out a gun and threatened to shoot Menon, before cooling down and signing!

States That Acceded After Independence...

JUNAGADH

The Hindu-majority coastal state of Junagadh was surrounded by India on three sides, but its main port was just over 300 nautical miles away from Pakistan. The Muslim ruler of Junagarh, Nawab Muhammad Mahabat Khan III, acceded to Pakistan against the wishes of his people. This led to a revolt, prompting the Indian army to intervene. The panicked nawab fled to Pakistan. A keen dog-lover, he also took 200 of his dogs with him! In February 1948, a plebiscite (general vote) was held, in which over 90 per cent of the local population voted in favour of accession to India.

Muhammad Mahabat Khan III

HYDERABAD

Mir Usman Ali

Hyderabad was among the richest, largest and most populous princely states. The Nizam of Hyderabad, Mir Usman Ali, wanted independence once the British left India and refused all offers for accession. He then allowed a paramilitary body called the 'Razakars' to seize control and come down heavily on anyone espousing accession. The situation turned extremely violent and India sent its troops to Hyderabad on 13 September 1948. In less than four days, the army had full control of the state. The Nizam finally relented. He banned the Razakars, blaming them for spreading terror in the state, and acceded to India.

War in Kashmir

The princely state that posed the biggest challenge for India was Jammu and Kashmir (J&K). Located on the northern tip of the country, it was even larger than Hyderabad, and was one of the most beautiful parts of the subcontinent. Unlike most other parts of India, J&K was largely Muslim-dominated. But its maharaja, Hari Singh, was a Hindu. Even though Kashmir, unlike Junagarh and Hyderabad, shared a border with both India and Pakistan, Hari Singh sought independence and refused to accede to either country. Instead, on 15 August 1947, the maharaja agreed to sign a standstill agreement with both countries, to allow the free movement of people and goods across the borders of his state. However, by September, relations with Pakistan began to deteriorate. Cross-border movement was suspended by Pakistan and essential supplies were blocked in order to apply pressure. There were also reports that Pakistan was preparing to send a large number of infiltrators into Kashmir, in a bid to force the state to accede to it.

The situation in the state was getting worse, but Hari Singh continued to cling on to his dream of independence. In October 1947, a large group of armed infiltrators launched a full-fledged invasion, swiftly making their way to Srinagar, in Kashmir. By the 25th, they were wreaking havoc in Baramulla, less than 60 km away from Srinagar. There was no time to waste. The maharaja took refuge in Jammu and requested the Indian government for urgent military assistance. The very next day, he acceded to India, and on the 27th, Indian planes made their way to Kashmir, carrying soldiers and supplies. Infuriated, Pakistan ordered its troops to launch a counteroffensive. Barely a few months had passed since Independence and India was already fighting a war.

Even as hostilities continued on the ground, in January 1948, on the advice of Lord Mountbatten, the Kashmir issue was taken to the United Nations (UN). India wanted the UN to help clear the illegal occupation of Kashmir by infiltrators loyal to Pakistan. However, Pakistan suggested that all armed forces should be withdrawn from the state and the people should be asked to vote on accession. It found many sympathizers in the UN and India began to regret its decision of going to the world body. Nevertheless, a Special Commission was set up to investigate the matter and after lengthy discussions, a ceasefire was ordered in January 1949. It established a Line of Control (LoC), allowing Pakistan to retain the parts of Kashmir it had occupied. The war came to an end, but neither nation was happy. Pakistan had failed to annexe the entire state, while the Indian army had been stopped in its tracks by the ceasefire and was unable to reclaim the annexed territory.

Another important person in the princely state of J&K was Sheikh Abdullah, a charismatic politician who, unlike Hari Singh, freely engaged with the people and was hugely popular. He had helped in founding a local party—the National Conference—and wanted a government of the people in Kashmir, instead of the maharaja's rule. After J&K acceded to India, Abdullah, who had been close friends with Nehru, was handed over the administration of the state. Together with his followers, he even assisted India during the war. Abdullah was a great believer in interfaith harmony and was against the idea of joining Muslim-dominated Pakistan. During the war and even after it, he continued to cement his power over the people of Kashmir. Soon after the ceasefire, Kashmir was opened to tourists. A few months later, Nehru, who was Kashmiri, took a historic trip. Everywhere he went, the crowds cheered him on. For a while it appeared that peace had truly returned to the state. However, as history shows, tensions were far from over (*see page 217*).

Making a Union

Accession was only the first step in remaking the map. By December 1947, Patel and Menon began the next—integration, that was, dissolving the states as individual entities and merging them with the Union of India. The situation was delicate. The rulers, who had already given up some rights in the process of accession, were now being asked to give up much more. However, Patel and Menon were helped in this pursuit by the people of the states who by and large wanted to become part of India, as well as friendly states who had come over on their side. Threatened by the possibility of mass revolt by their subjects or lured by the other states that had integrated, many rulers fell in line. In return for integration, they were allowed to retain their titles, palaces and other personal properties. They were also offered a 'privy purse'—an annual allowance. The size of this allowance varied drastically based on factors like the revenue earned by the state, the legacy of the ruling dynasty, etc. By the end of 1949, the map had been remade. Over 500 princely states merged with the Union of India and were reorganized to create new administrative units. This was among the greatest achievements of Independent India—one for which there are few parallels in history.

Another Reorganization

India has always been a land of many languages and the Congress supported this diversity. Long before Independence, it had committed itself to the idea of creating states based on languages. However, in 1947, India had been divided along tense communal lines and its leaders worried. Would dividing the country further, on the basis of language, threaten its fragile unity in the aftermath of Partition?

While the Indian leadership did not want to risk another division, by 1948–49, people in many parts of India, from Marathi to Malayalam speakers, were already campaigning for the creation of states on the basis of language. One of the most forceful movements was by Telugu speakers. They submitted petitions and representations, and organized street marches and fasts for the formation of an Andhra state, made up of the Telugu districts in what was then the state of Madras (now Tamil Nadu). The central government continued to resist, but this only worsened the agitation. On 19 October 1952, with the blessings of thousands of Telugu speakers and the movement's leadership, a man named Potti Sriramulu began a fast-unto-death. Frantic telegrams were sent to the government. Strikes were organized and angry mobs were shouting slogans against leaders like Nehru, for ignoring their demand for a separate state for Telugu speakers. By December, the movement became impossible to ignore. But before the Indian leadership could act upon the matter, Sriramulu died and all hell broke loose. Protestors went on a rampage, destroying lakhs of rupees worth of state property, attacking government offices and defacing trains. Many were killed in police firings. Finally, on 19 December 1952, the demand for

Andhra was accepted and the new state was inaugurated on 1 October 1953.

The creation of Andhra intensified similar demands by other language speakers. Much against its will, the government set up the States Reorganisation Commission in 1953. Over the next two years, members of the commission travelled throughout the country and in November 1956, the States Reorganisation Act was passed. The map of Independent India was reorganized once again to create fourteen states and six Union territories administered by the centre. Among other changes, southern India was divided into four states: Andhra Pradesh for Telugu speakers, Madras for Tamil speakers, Kerala for Malayalam speakers and Mysore for Kannada speakers, while the Hindi-speaking belt was divided into Rajasthan, Uttar Pradesh, Madhya Pradesh and Bihar.

When India was first being divided on the basis of language, its leaders were worried while its critics were gleeful. Many believed that no nation could exist without a 'common voice' and one that speaks so many different languages was bound to fall apart. Yet, India has thrived in its multilingualism. By going against the wisdom of critics and not imposing a common language, it has allowed its people the comfort of speaking their own language while still remaining Indian.

Other Colonialists

Even though the British left in 1947, the French and the Portuguese continued to stick on to their colonies in India. Faced with rising nationalist anger against their regime, the French finally handed over their territories to India in

November 1954. They had controlled three slivers of land in the south, most well-known of which was the port of Pondicherry (now Puducherry).

The Portuguese, however, were not willing to give up their territories, which were located along the mid-western coast of India. The most well-known of these was Goa. For a decade, India attempted to non-violently persuade the Portuguese to give up their territories. But, by 1961, its patience was wearing thin. On the morning of 18 December 1961, Indian troops entered Goa, and in a little over a day, the Portuguese surrendered their colonies. The Goans rejoiced and even helped the troops in the mission, and 19 December came to be celebrated as 'Goa Liberation Day'.

An Ever-changing Map

In the years since Independence, the map of India has been remade several times to accommodate the desires of different groups of its people. That is why we have so many more states today than we had in 1956. Yet, it's important to note that so far, no part has fallen away.

Remaking India's Map

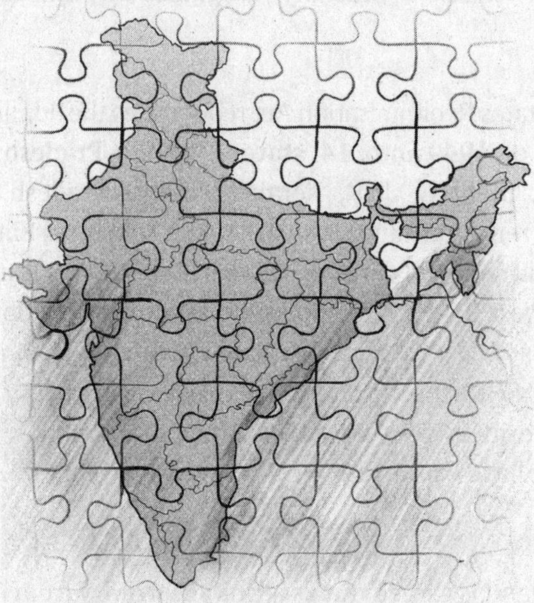

1949

Reorganization of British provinces and princely states ends with the creation of various administrative units: Assam, Bihar, Bombay, Madhya Pradesh, Madras, Orissa, East Punjab (British province of Punjab), Uttar Pradesh, West Bengal, Hyderabad, J&K, Madhya Bharat, Mysore, Patiala and East Punjab States Union (PEPSU), Rajasthan, Saurashtra, Travancore, Ajmer, Bhopal, Bilaspur, Coorg state, Delhi, Himachal Pradesh, Kutch, Manipur, Tripura, Vindhya Pradesh.

1954
The French colony of Pondicherry (renamed Puducherry) is transferred to the Union of the India and becomes a Union Territory—officially recognized by France in 1962

1956
The States Reorganisation Act reorganizes the administrative units of 1949 into **14 states**: Andhra Pradesh, Assam, Bihar, Bombay, J&K, Kerala, Madhya Pradesh, Madras (later renamed Tamil Nadu), Mysore (renamed Karnataka), Orissa (renamed Odisha), Punjab, Rajasthan, Uttar Pradesh and West Bengal, and **6 Union Territories**: Andaman and Nicobar Islands, Delhi, Manipur (became a state in 1972), Tripura (became a state 1972), Himachal Pradesh (became a state in 1971), Laccadive, Minicoy & Amindivi Islands. These have continued to evolve over the years

1957
Nagaland is carved out as a Union Territory from Assam (it became a state in 1963)

1960
Bombay is split into Gujarat and Maharashtra and Bombay city (now Mumbai) becomes the capital of Maharashtra

1961
The Portuguese colonies of Goa, Dadra and Nagar Haveli, Daman and Diu are surrendered to the Union of India and become Union Territories (Goa became a state in 1987 while Daman and Diu were merged with Dadra and Nagar Haveli in 2019)

1966

- Haryana is carved out as a state from Punjab
- Northern districts of Punjab merged with Himachal Pradesh

1972

- Meghalaya is carved out as a state from Assam
- Mizoram is carved out as a Union Territory from Assam (it became a state in 1987)
- Arunachal Pradesh (formerly known as the North-East Frontier Agency) becomes a Union Territory (it became a state in 1987)

1975

Sikkim joins the Union of India

2000

- Chhattisgarh is carved out as a state from Madhya Pradesh
- Uttaranchal (renamed Uttarakhand) is carved out as a state from Uttar Pradesh
- Jharkhand is carved out as a state from Bihar

2014

Telangana is carved out as a state from Andhra Pradesh

2019

J&K is split into the Union Territories of Jammu and Kashmir and Ladakh

4

Ideas of India

On a cold winter morning, on 9 December 1946, over 200 Indian leaders met at the Central Hall of the Parliament House in Delhi. Chosen on the basis of the elections held in the British provinces that year, these leaders formed the Constituent Assembly, a body that was going to create India's Constitution—the supreme law that would influence most aspects of its independent life in the coming years.

The hall was decorated elegantly with bright lamps and a sense of eagerness filled the air. It was a historic moment. On the first day an inaugural address was made, and all the members registered their presence. The press and visitors viewed the proceedings from galleries at the top of the hall, while All India Radio broadcasted them for listeners outside. Over the next three years, the members would meet in eleven sessions to draw up the Constitution. This incredibly weighty work didn't get any easier because of the tumultuous times they faced.

First meeting of the Constituent Assembly

Only Indians!

The constituent assembly was made up entirely of Indians. Even though Lord Wavell, who was the Viceroy of India back in 1946, wanted to play a role in it, he was politely told to stay away.

When the assembly began its work in 1946, it only knew that freedom was on the horizon. However, it didn't know the exact date. So one can imagine the worry when it was decided that India would be free by August 1947—Independence was so close, yet work on the Constitution was far from complete! It didn't help that the Muslim League was insisting on a separate Muslim-majority nation of Pakistan and communal violence raged in different parts of the country. Many members of the Assembly, who had been close friends with leaders of the League, were disappointed that the party had stuck to its demand for Partition and boycotted the momentous work of framing a constitution for free India—a dream that had been common to both communities for the longest time. And then came the carnage in the aftermath of Partition. The grief and the trauma were worsened by the assassination of Mahatma Gandhi in January 1948. Still, the assembly plodded on.

Talking it Out

In framing the laws that would govern free India, the assembly was laying the foundation to revolutionary change that would transform the country. Here was a golden chance to undo age-old social and economic injustice and empower the masses. The members of the assembly engaged in spirited debates, discussions and arguments over what kind of nation India should be, the values it should uphold, the language it should speak and the political and economic systems it should follow.

Even though the constituent assembly was dominated by the Congress, it didn't speak in one voice. The members belonged to different parts of India and held diverse views. Some were inspired by socialism while others defended landlordism. Some were close to communal parties while others were assertively secular. There were various members representing different caste and religious groups. The exchanges between them have been documented in eleven bulky volumes that exceed 1000 pages! These not only reveal the verbosity, intelligence, insight and passion of the assembly members but also many competing ideas of India, held by them.

Some members wanted a more powerful central government while others favoured the states. Some wanted special privileges for minorities and women who had suffered much discrimination while others worried about how this would affect the quest for equality. Some wanted seats in the union and state legislatures to be reserved for lower castes and tribal groups. Much time was also spent on the issue of language. After a series of pitched battles, the assembly chose Hindi as the official language of the Union of India, but for ease of transition from British to Indian rule, for fifteen years from the commencement of the Constitution, English would continue to be used along with Hindi for all official communication between the centre and the states.

English in India

During the 1960s, when Hindi was declared the national language under the Official Languages Act, large-scale riots erupted in Tamil Nadu. Many other non-Hindi-speaking states also protested against the imposition of Hindi. The intensity of the agitation, particularly in Tamil Nadu, alarmed the central government and ensured that English continued as an official language. Today, India has among the largest numbers of English speakers in the world. 'Indian' English has contributed several new words, such as 'jugaad', 'dadagiri' and 'chutney' to English dictionaries, while Indian authors writing in English have won some of the most prestigious awards for English literature, including the International Booker Prize.

Constitutions of various countries were also carefully examined to determine the features that were best suited for India. For example, the parliamentary system was inspired by the UK, while the American constitution inspired the Fundamental Rights.

Putting it Together

A country as diverse and talkative as India was making its Constitution, so lengthy deliberations were to be expected. But how was the actual work of documenting the Constitution even happening in the midst of all that talk?

The herculean task of determining different subjects to be included in the Constitution and preparing detailed reports on these was assigned to several different committees. These committees were made up of members drawn from the assembly and those helping them. For example, there was a committee looking exclusively into Fundamental Rights that had twelve members from the assembly and was headed by J.B. Kriplani. Similarly, there was another committee working on tribal areas in the Northeast, which was headed by assembly member Gopinath Bordoloi. Leaders like Jawaharlal Nehru and Sardar Patel headed more than one committee and worked steadfastly to ensure the smooth functioning of the assembly. Once their reports were ready, the committees would put them before the larger assembly. After they were debated, discussed and revised, the Drafting Committee, headed by B.R. Ambedkar, did the gruelling work of putting it all together.

B.R. Ambedkar and the Drafting Committee

B.R. Ambedkar

Considered an 'untouchable' by India's caste-ridden society, Bhimrao Ramji Ambedkar faced injustice from his very first day at school. He and his brother had to sit outside their classroom on gunny sacks that they brought from home. The teachers ignored them. The other children did not play with them and they were not even allowed to get drinking water from the well. Yet, Ambedkar's brilliance was hard to ignore. Sayajirao Gaekwad III, the Maharaja of Baroda, awarded him a scholarship to study abroad and Ambedkar went on to get four doctorates and a degree in law. One of the most brilliant and scholarly men of the time, Ambedkar was invited to lead the Drafting Committee, even though he did not belong to the Congress party. Under his leadership, the committee drafted the entire Constitution piece by piece, making legal sense of all the inputs from assembly members. It is for this reason that B.R. Ambedkar is called the Father of the Indian Constitution.

Any mention of this powerful committee would be incomplete without crediting the work of the Constitutional Advisor B.N. Rau and the Chief Drafting Officer S.N.Mukherjee. An expert on constitutions, Rau prepared the initial draft while Mukherjee documented it in the correct legal language.

This text was then discussed by the Drafting Committee, before being presented to the assembly.

Making it Public

In 1948, a detailed draft of the Constitution was published for the public and people were invited to send in their views. Hundreds of responses poured in from all corners of the country. India's remarkable diversity and divides were on display again. Hindu groups, such as the All-India Varnashrama Swarajya Sangh, wanted the Constitution to be based on ancient Hindu works. They recommended the prohibition of cow slaughter and the closing down of slaughterhouses. Lower-caste groups demanded an end to oppression by upper-caste people and reservation of seats in various government bodies. Linguistic minorities wanted the freedom of speech in their mother tongue and the reorganization of India along linguistic lines. Bodies such as the District Teachers Guild of Vizianagaram and the Central Jewish Board of Bombay wanted adequate representation on all public bodies including legislatures, among other things.

Thousands of claims and demands were received from the public and all of them were reviewed by the Secretariat of the Assembly before being deliberated further.

Finally, a Constitution

After several rounds of deliberations, the assembly adopted the final draft of the Constitution on 26 November 1949. With over 1,40,000 words, it was one of the longest constitutions ever adopted. Framing it had been 'a task of tremendous magnitude' for it covered a population of over 30 crore people, who belonged to different communities, spoke in different languages and were deeply divided on the basis of religion, caste, class and gender. When the constituent assembly began its work, the land itself was divided into British provinces and over 500 princely states. However, by the time the Constitution had been written, the provinces and an overwhelming majority of the princely states were one nation with one constitution.

On 24 January 1950, the constituent assembly met for the last time. It decided that 'Jana Gana Mana' would be the national anthem of India, elected Dr Rajendra Prasad to be the President of the country and signed three copies of the Constitution. The first two copies in English and Hindi were handwritten in exquisite calligraphy by Prem Behari Narain Raizada and Vasant Krishna Vaidya. They featured beautiful illustrations by a team of artists led by the famous painter Nandalal Bose. The third copy was printed in English.

President Rajendra Prasad leaves for the first Republic Day in an open buggy

Two days later, on 26 January, India celebrated its first Republic Day. The Constitution came into effect, replacing the earlier, colonial-era laws under which India had been governed till then. The last official connection with British rule was over. India was now a sovereign republic where power was held by the people and their elected representatives. Ambedkar, who had experienced the worst and best of India, cautioned people against resorting to anarchy for meeting their demands. He advised them to think twice before submitting to powerful leadership and asked them to strive for democracy in all spheres of life. Mere political democracy, exercised through the right to vote, would remain futile if there was no equality in the social and economic life of India.

Amending the Constitution

The Constitution empowered the people of India with freedom that came with certain Fundamental Rights. It was the responsibility of the government of the day, watched over by the courts, to uphold these rights. And if these rights were violated, people could go to the courts to enforce them—and indeed, they were quick to do so! Barely two weeks after the Constitution came into force, the Bombay High Court released prisoners who had been detained for eight long months without trial under the draconian Bombay Safety Measures Act. The Constitution had given these prisoners a powerful tool against their detention. Several other cases were being filed throughout the country and the courts were regularly hauling up the government for running afoul of constitutional provisions on various grounds. Judicial interpretation of the various Fundamental Rights was making it difficult for the government to function smoothly. In response to this, the government passed the first amendment to the Constitution in June 1951—barely a year after it had been put into effect. It made several changes to the articles on Fundamental Rights and was passed despite tremendous opposition both within and outside the Parliament. Since then, the original constitution has been amended over 100 times by different governments in power.

* * *

About the Constitution

The Constitution is a long document that runs into hundreds of pages that are currently divided into 25 parts, 12 schedules and more than 460 articles! It lays down the laws that govern India—everything from how the government is to be formed to the rights that India's citizens have.

The PREAMBLE is an introduction to the Constitution. Beginning with the words, 'We, the people of India . . .' it tells the world the ideals of India—the kind of nation and society it wants to be.

Sovereign: *It decides its own policies and no other country can tell it what to do.*

Socialist: *It strives to reduce income inequalities and improve the lives of its people by promoting economic justice and opposing exploitation.*

Secular: *It does not have any state religion. People have the freedom to follow their own religion and people of all religions are equal.*

Democratic: *People exercise power by electing representatives to the government who are responsible to them.*

Republic: *Power lies with the people and not a hereditary monarch whose rule is imposed upon them.*

DIRECTIVE PRINCIPLES guide governments in making policies for the social and economic welfare of the people, such as ensuring equal pay for men and women, good working conditions and better healthcare.

FUNDAMENTAL RIGHTS are basic and essential rights given to all citizens, such as the right to equality, which ensures that all laws apply to everyone equally, or the right against exploitation, which abolishes forced labour and child labour. These rights are legally enforceable. So people can go to court if they feel that their fundamental rights have been violated. However, Fundamental Rights come with limits and can be restricted during an emergency or to preserve public order or national security.

FUNDAMENTAL DUTIES are duties expected of each citizen of India, such as abiding by the Constitution, respecting the national flag and the national anthem, promoting brotherhood, preserving our nation's heritage, protecting the environment, etc.

Structure of the Government

India has a FEDERAL GOVERNMENT. This means powers are shared between the central and state governments and both of them make laws and policies. However, the subjects on which they are allowed to do so vary. The Constitution lays down 3 different lists of subjects:

Parliament house

***Union List**: exclusively under the control of the central government*

***State List**: exclusively under the control of state governments*

***Concurrent List**: both the central and state governments can make laws and policies*

LEGISLATURE makes laws and policies for the nation

***Union Legislature** (central govt): divided into Lok Sabha (elected directly by the people) and Rajya Sabha (elected by members of the Vidhan Sabhas. A few are chosen by the President.)*

***State Legislature** (state govt): divided into Vidhan Sabha (elected directly by the people) and Vidhan Parishad (elected by members of the Vidhan Sabha, various local bodies, graduates and teachers in the state. A few are chosen by the governor of the state.)*

EXECUTIVE implements laws and policies to run the nation with the help of a large body of government officials. It is made up of the:

President: *Symbolic head of Executive*

Prime Minister (PM): *Active head of Executive*

Council of Ministers: *Team chosen by the PM*

JUDICIARY interprets and applies the laws to administer justice. It is headed by the Supreme Court, below which are the high courts in various states and finally, the lower courts in various districts.

5

The Greatest Experiment in Democracy

Democracy was one of the greatest unifying ideas espoused by India's Constitution. It empowered all Indians above a fixed age with the right to vote and elect a government that would be answerable to them. But most of them were clueless about it! Even though elections had been held under British rule, only property owners and taxpayers were allowed to vote. A large number of Indians had never voted before. Compounding this problem was the fact that a majority of them could neither read nor write. How was one going to make them aware of this new power that the Constitution had given them? Would they be able to vote? Some people were questioning India's Constitution for giving voting rights to its large and uneducated population, others were curious and nervous about the outcome of this exercise. No wonder then, that the first elections in Independent India were being touted as the greatest experiment in democracy anywhere in the world. The formidable task of conducting this experiment fell on the Election Commission—an independent constitutional authority, appointed by the President, that was headed by the chief election commissioner.

Power of the Vote

Throughout history, people in many parts of the world have struggled for the right to vote, which was usually restricted to men with power and privilege. For example, in the United States, women were not allowed to vote until 1920. Similarly, in Australia, indigenous people only started voting from 1962.

Getting Election Ready

Sukumar Sen—India's first chief election commissioner—was an award-winning mathematician and a tough officer who believed in strictly following rules. When he came into office in March 1950, he had a stupendous task before him. Over 17 crore people, twenty-one years old and above (changed to eighteen years and above in later years), most of whom could neither read nor write, had to be identified, named and registered for voting! This was merely the first step. The entire design of the election—from party symbols to ballot papers and ballot boxes—had to be easy to understand for this electorate. Moreover, polling stations had to be identified and set up for a population that was spread over lakhs of square kilometres—from remote villages in the hills to small islands in the Indian Ocean. To top it all, money was tight and the commission had to monitor expenses closely. Naturally, this was too much work for one man! Helping Sen in this phenomenal task were two regional commissioners and an army made up of lakhs of election workers—all of whom were recruited in the run-up to the first election.

Sukumar Sen: India's first chief election commissioner at work

Throughout 1951, newspapers, films and All-India Radio were used to educate the people about the Constitution, the preparation of voting lists and the purpose and process of voting. Election workers went from house to house drawing up lists of voters that were eventually typed out as electoral rolls. Pictorial symbols drawn from daily life, such as a pair of bullocks, a hut and an elephant, were used as party symbols so people could recognize them easily. At polling stations, each party was allotted a separate ballot box bearing its symbol, so that voters could simply drop their paper into the ballot box of the party they wanted to vote for. To prevent people from voting more than once, an indelible ink was applied to each voter's finger after voting. This would not go away for a week. Bridges were constructed over rivers to reach remote villages and naval vessels were used to reach islands in the Indian Ocean. Bit by bit, the Election Commission solved the problems.

Symbols of various political parties that contested in the first elections

Meanwhile, different political parties campaigned for votes. They conducted large public meetings, did door-to-door canvassing and used various visual media. From walls to street corners, party symbols could be seen everywhere. In some places—even on the backs of stray cows!

Women in some places in northern India hesitated in sharing their names with election workers preparing voter lists. Much of this hesitance was a result of age-old male dominance. Instead of giving their names the women wanted to register themselves as some man's mother, wife or sister. Sen courted heavy criticism when he refused to allow them to vote unless they shared their names. But his refusal prompted them to have their names registered and vote for the first time in the next election.

The Contestants

Democratic India's first election had a dazzling array of parties reflecting its diverse interests. All of them had one common opponent—the Indian National Congress led by Jawaharlal Nehru—and they all blamed it for not doing enough to secure the interests of the different groups of people they were representing. The Socialist Party and others who represented the interests of the workers and peasants claimed that the Congress was neglecting the poor and favouring the wealthy. The Jana Sangh that sought to win over the Hindus—India's largest religious group—accused the Congress of appeasing the Muslims. The Scheduled Castes Federation attacked the Congress for doing little to uplift the lower castes.

The ruling Congress indeed had a lot to deal with. In addition to its opponents, it faced several other pressing problems—angry refugees from Pakistan in the aftermath of the Partition, issues around the reorganization of states and widespread poverty and inequality . . . Despite these concerns, Nehru set off on a nine-week-long, historic election campaign that saw him covering over 40,000 km by air, car, train and even by boat. In giant rallies, he spoke against landlordism, communalism and untouchability, urging people to vote without fear. He was seen as Mahatma Gandhi's successor, and wherever he went, people flocked to see and hear him, even if they did not always agree with him. No one could deny his extraordinary popularity.

The First Elections

Finally, after months of preparation, India was ready to hold its first election to fill 4500 seats. Of these, about 500 were for the Lok Sabha at the centre, while the rest were for the Vidhan Sabhas (state assemblies). Polling began on 25 October 1951 and went on, across different parts of the country, till 21 February 1952. About 60 per cent of the registered voters exercised their voting rights.

Independent India's first voter

The first Indians to cast their votes on 25 October belonged to the Chini district in Himachal Pradesh. Among them was the schoolteacher Shyam Saran Negi, who became Independent India's first voter, before heading off for the polling duty that had been assigned to him.

India's first elections

Source: Report on the First General Election in India, 1951-52

2,24,000
Polling stations constructed

3,80,000
Reams of paper used to print the voting lists

2,80,000
People helping the election officers

3,89,816
Phials of indelible ink used to mark voters' fingers

20,00,000
Steel ballot boxes

56,000
Officers chosen to supervise the elections

2,24,000
Policemen put on duty to maintain law and order

1250
Election offences, such as trying to vote more than once, taking ballot papers out of polling stations and canvassing close to polling stations.

Voting day turned into a festival as people arrived at polling booths dressed in their finest clothes. Many defied personal challenges to vote. In Madurai, a 110-year-old man came to vote, propped up on either side by a great-grandson. In Ambala, a deaf and hunchbacked woman didn't let disability stop her from voting. In Hyderabad, the nizam, who at one point wanted to remain independent of India, was among the first to vote. In the Mizo Hills, tribal people reached polling booths after walking for days through wild jungles and camping at night amid songs and community dances. India's incredible experiment with democracy had made a fantastic debut.

People defied disability to come to polling stations for voting

When votes were finally counted, the Congress had a comfortable win all across the country. However, over 50 per cent of the voters had also voted for other parties. Dismissed as too uneducated for voting rights, ordinary Indians had shown their ability to vote thoughtfully.

Election Season

Free and fair elections—where people are able to vote for a representative of their choice without any pressure and every vote counts—form the bedrock of democracy. Every time an election fails to be free and fair, questions are raised about the fate of democracy. Unfortunately, this has become increasingly common in India.

As the number of voters and political parties has increased, the cost of election campaigns has also gone up exponentially. Political parties spend large sums of money on publicity, travel arrangements for popular leaders, etc., to woo voters. Those who are unable to do this may fail to get sufficient visibility and support. With so much money riding on campaigns, parties are often accused of using all kinds of means to win. This endangers free and fair elections.

Allegations of election fraud, such as illegally changing the result of an election by producing a false record of the number of votes (vote rigging) have become common over the years. Reports of intimidating voters through poll violence have also increased. It is no longer unusual to find politicians with criminal backgrounds. Many parties play upon caste and religious sentiments to win over voters. Candidates are often fielded based on their caste, creed and community instead of their accomplishments, ability and merits.

Over the years, many people have claimed that democracy has been eroded by politics that only concerns itself with winning elections and not with improving the lives of those it represents. Yet, voter turnout has steadily increased since the first elections and people have braved grave threats to exercise their right to vote. In fact, India is possibly the only large democracy in the world where the oppressed and marginalized have been voting in higher numbers than the privileged groups. As long as elections continue to be held regularly and people continue to vote, India will continue to be called a democracy—and where there is democracy, there is always hope for people to prevail.

Lok Sabha (LS) elections in India

1952

- First election in Independent India
- Congress led by Jawaharlal Nehru wins a majority in parliament

1957

- Second LS elections
- Congress led by Jawaharlal Nehru wins a majority in parliament

1962

- Third LS elections
- Congress led by Jawaharlal Nehru wins a majority in parliament

1964
Jawaharlal Nehru dies, is replaced by Lal Bahadur Shastri

1966
Lal Bahadur Shastri dies, is replaced by Indira Gandhi

1967
- Fourth LS elections
- Congress led by Indira Gandhi wins a majority in parliament, but is shocked by the decline in its seats.

1969
Indira Gandhi is expelled from the Congress as several members turn against her. She forms Congress (R) [R for Requisitionist] but remains in power with the support of other parties.

1970
Lok Sabha is dissolved for the first time without completing the full term of 5 years

1971
- Fifth LS Elections
- Congress (R) led by Indira Gandhi wins a majority in Parliament, is called Congress (I) [I for Indira] and eventually, just the Congress.

1975
Indira Gandhi imposes an emergency and cancels elections (*also see page 144*)

1977

- Sixth LS Elections
- A coalition government, made up of several different parties, comes to power for the first time, with Morarji Desai as the PM

1979

Charan Singh replaces Morarji Desai as PM, but loses support and continues as caretaker PM

1980

- Seventh LS Elections
- Congress led by Indira Gandhi wins a majority

1982

Electronic Voting Machines (EVMs) are first used during a by-election in Kerala (used throughout the country from 2004)

1984

- Indira Gandhi is assassinated, replaced by her son Rajiv Gandhi
- Eighth LS Elections
- Congress led by Rajiv Gandhi wins the highest majority ever in Parliament

1989

- Ninth LS Elections
- A coalition government comes to power, with V.P. Singh as the PM
- Voting age is lowered from 21 to 18 years

1990

Chandrashekhar replaces V.P. Singh as PM, but loses support and continues as caretaker PM.

1991

- Rajiv Gandhi is assassinated
- Tenth LS Elections
- A coalition government led by Congress comes to power, with Narasimha Rao as PM

1996

- Eleventh LS Elections
- No party has a clear majority. BJP led by A.B. Vajpayee tries forming a government, but does not succeed
- A coalition government called United Front comes to power, with H.D. Deve Gowda as PM

1997

I.K. Gujral replaces H.D. Deve Gowda as PM

1998

- Twelfth LS Elections
- A coalition government called National Democratic Alliance (NDA) led by the BJP comes to power, with A.B. Vajpayee as PM

1999

- NDA loses majority
- Thirteenth LS Elections
- NDA led by BJP returns to power, with A.B. Vajpayee as PM

2004

- Fourteenth LS Elections
- A coalition government called United Progressive Alliance (UPA) led by the Congress comes to power, with Manmohan Singh as PM

2009

- Fifteenth LS Elections
- UPA led by Congress returns to power, with Manmohan Singh as PM

2013

'None of the Above' (NOTA) voting option is introduced

2014

- Sixteenth LS Elections
- BJP led by Narendra Modi wins a majority

2019

- Seventeenth LS Elections
- Transgender voters vote under their chosen gender identity, after a Supreme Court verdict in 2014 officially declares them the 'third gender'
- BJP led by Narendra Modi returns to power

6

A Taste of Defeat

In 1946, as India was getting ready for Independence, neighbouring China was in the midst of a bitter conflict between rival groups: the communists led by Mao Zedong and the nationalists led by Chiang Kai-shek. By the time India finished drafting its Constitution in 1949, power had been seized by the communists. Unlike India, that had chosen the path of democracy and given its people the right to choose their government, China was now a communist nation firmly in the grip of the Chinese Communist Party led by Mao. Both India and China were ancient Asian civilizations with a history going back thousands of years. China was a powerful country and newly independent India was not in a position to make adversaries. So, despite the differences between them, democratic India chose to befriend communist China.

India was the first country to officially recognize the People's Republic of China under Mao and also supported its attempts to be admitted to the United Nations (UN). The Indian embassy in China continued to function under the serving ambassador K.M. Panikkar, who sent in favourable reports after meeting Mao in May 1950. But what happened next left India in a deep dilemma . . .

Mao Zedong shaking hands with Jawaharlal Nehru

Democracy in India has also made room for various communist parties to contest elections. In 1957, the Communist Party of India won a majority in Kerala and formed the first democratically elected communist government in the world!

Annexation of Tibet

In October 1950, China annexed Tibet—a mountainous country in the Himalayas, located between India and China. India now shared a vast border with China. In the west, this border ran along Ladakh, touching both Tibet and Sinkiang in China while, in the east, it ran along Arunachal Pradesh (formerly the North East Frontier Agency). Most of this border was a cold, inhospitable and sparsely populated region that was unmarked and unsurveyed. But in 1914, the British had signed a Treaty with Tibet that recognized the McMahon Line running across the crest of the Himalayas in the east as the boundary between Tibet and British India. China had long disagreed on the McMahon Line and India feared that having annexed Tibet, it may violate this boundary. The voices warning Jawaharlal Nehru against the Chinese grew more strident. They urged the Prime Minister to be aware of the danger and enter a military pact with democratic western powers in a bid to protect India's frontiers.

However, in the early 1950s, China appeared to be favourably disposed towards India. In an effort to build goodwill, India and China signed a wide-ranging agreement in April 1954. Among other things, Tibet was recognized as a part of China and the countries made a joint declaration outlining five principles of peaceful co-existence (*panch sheel*), which included mutual non-aggression and respect for each other's territorial integrity. At the end of the year, Nehru visited China for the first time and discussed border questions. The trip appeared to have gone well, for the Prime Minister returned with an assurance that the Chinese wanted to maintain friendly relations with India.

Two years later, on the 2500th birth anniversary of the Buddha, Chinese leader Chou En-lai visited India together with the Dalai and Panchen Lamas of Tibet. During the course of the trip, the Dalai Lama escaped his Chinese minders to talk to Nehru and informed him of the revolt that was brewing in Tibet against Chinese occupiers. When Nehru questioned Chou about the situation, he was told that there had indeed been some unfortunate incidents but these would be looked into. Reasonably assured, Nehru let the matter rest. Meanwhile, away from each other's eyes, India and China were working on protecting their territorial interests. The only difference was that while India concentrated on the McMahon Line in the east, China was steadily expanding its footprint on the western border.

Mounting Tensions

In 1957, evidence of road-building within its territory came to India's notice. A year later, an official Chinese magazine printed a map that showed large parts of Ladakh and Arunachal Pradesh within China. A highway had been built, linking Sinkiang in China to Tibet, that passed through thousands of kilometres of Indian territory. India was appalled. Nehru and

Chou began exchanging letters that made it clear that China did not recognize the border between India and Tibet. Even though India had ample evidence to support its claims, it fell on deaf ears.

In August and October 1959, violent border clashes prompted India to adopt a 'forward policy' and begin setting up a series of small posts in the border areas. However, no definitive steps were taken to prepare the army. Meanwhile, in September 1959, the Government of India released its correspondence with the Chinese over the past five years. The extent of the border dispute and differences between the countries were now publicly known. Nationalist sentiments were aroused. People were angry and wanted India to take a strong stand against China.

In November 1959, as the face-off between Chinese troops and the Tibetan rebels became intense, the Dalai Lama—Tibet's spiritual leader and head of state—fled to India with a small band of followers. Much to China's resentment, they were granted asylum and welcomed by large sections of the Indian public. However, India declined to go to war with China over Tibet's freedom. It even assured the Chinese that while the exiled Tibetan leader would be treated with respect, he was not expected to carry out any political activities against China from Indian soil and that India had no intention of interfering with Tibet's internal happenings. But China refused to buy this argument.

Dalai Lama and the Potala Palace in Tibet

Despite all these happenings, Nehru and his defence minister V.K. Krishna Menon continued to believe that the dispute with China could be resolved without war. The correspondence between Nehru and Chou continued and in April 1960 the two leaders met at a summit in New Delhi. But talks failed. The Chinese were determined to retain their gains, especially along the western border. Yet, it was hoped that war could be avoided and official exchanges continued between the two governments. Meanwhile, clashes on the border became more regular. In July 1962, there were clashes in the Galwan Valley of Ladakh along the western border, and in September, at Dhola, along the eastern border. Finally, on the night between 19 and 20 October, war broke out, as the Chinese invaded both the eastern and western borders.

An Unequal War

Waves of Chinese troops marched into Indian territory under the cover of thunderous fire power. They outnumbered and overwhelmed India's defences. Having occupied Tibet, they had successfully fought off Tibetan rebels in the inhospitable Himalayan geography and unlike Indian troops, were used to warfare in the high mountains. Troop movement was also easier as they descended towards India, whereas the Indians had to ascend steep mountains with no proper roads to reach the border.

The war exposed India's vulnerability. Its troops were hopelessly ill-equipped and, in the absence of road connectivity, depended on air drops for supplies. The Chinese overran Indian defences with remarkable ease. Left with no other option, India finally reached out to the US for Western arms. By November, transport planes carrying arms and ammunition began to arrive. In an impassioned speech in Parliament, Nehru bitterly criticized the Chinese betrayal.

In the meantime, a brief lull in hostilities was broken by yet another Chinese offensive in November 1962. Despite instances of spirited defence, Indian troops could not hold up. Towards the end of November, the Chinese were poised to enter the plains of Assam and residents were seized by panic. But on 22 November, without any warning, China declared a ceasefire and its troops retreated to their positions before the war.

Why did the Chinese withdraw so suddenly? Some believed that this was because all parties in India, including the communists, were now firmly supporting the Indian government. Others said that supplies of Western arms had deterred the Chinese. Another important consideration was the change in season. Winter was setting in and soon the Himalayas would be covered in snow. This would make it difficult for supplies to reach the Chinese troops fighting on Indian plains.

On Republic Day in 1963, before a packed audience at the National Stadium in New Delhi, the legendary Indian singer Lata Mangeshkar performed the song 'Aye Mere Watan Ke Logon', commemorating the Indian soldiers who died in the war against China. It went on to become one of India's most famous patriotic songs.

A Massive Loss

Even though it ended hostilities, China retained large territories in Ladakh that it had captured before the war and left little doubt over its military superiority. India, on the other hand, suffered its first defeat and was left deeply wounded. Thousands of Indian soldiers were either dead or injured.

In the aftermath of the war, many senior army officials had to retire, while the defence minister V.K. Krishna Menon was removed from his position. As Prime Minister, Nehru had witnessed many challenges. However, the loss to China was seen as his greatest failure and the humiliation was all-pervasive. Many leaders in the West mocked him for requesting Western arms even though he had refused to join the Western democracies and had instead founded the Non-Aligned Movement (*see page XX*). Meanwhile, in August 1963, the opposition introduced the first no-confidence motion in India's parliamentary history, declaring that it longer trusted Nehru's government and wanted it out of office. Even though the Congress had a majority and was able to easily defeat the motion, the criticism unleashed upon Nehru was seething. Many, in his own party, had begun to question his authority.

The defeat made India realize how unsafe its borders were, prompting a deep need to modernize its defences. Since then, India has been investing heavily in strengthening its military might.

For a long time after the war, India and China suspended all exchanges. But as both countries grew in global importance, they could not afford to ignore each other. By the mid-1970s, exchanges resumed and grew stronger with each passing decade. Today, the countries have become major trade partners, importing goods worth billions of dollars from each other. That's why, despite the unresolved border dispute and ongoing stand-offs at the border, there is hope that the neighbours might find ways to overcome this essential tension between them.

Azad Krishna Chaturvedi was just a boy when the war broke out, but the memories of that time are hard to forget. Every time he stepped out, he could see people gathered around radios on the street, eagerly awaiting updates on the war, hanging on to every word uttered by Jawaharlal Nehru and discussing the situation on the border. 'The Prime Minister's agony was hard to miss. Listeners would sometimes cry after hearing the broadcast. Even street-dwellers were making donations for the war effort.' The loss in that war was soul-crushing. 'The nation was almost doomed. The euphoria of freedom had been soured by bitter reality.' Intensely moved by the scenes around him, Chaturvedi joined the army in 1967, and retired as a colonel in 2001.

Major Wars Fought by Independent India

Apart from the war with China, India has also fought some other major wars—primarily with Pakistan.

1947–1948: Indo-Pak War (*see page 33*)
Pakistani and Indian forces clash over Kashmir. The UN intervenes and negotiates a ceasefire that establishes a Line of Control (LoC) between both countries.

1965: Indo-Pak War
Pakistani and Indian forces clash over Kashmir. The UN negotiates a ceasefire and the USSR mediates. Both countries agree to withdraw forces from captured

territories, resume diplomatic ties and refrain from interfering in each other's internal affairs.

1971: Indo-Pak War (*see page 16*)
India defeats Pakistan, leading to the creation of Bangladesh

1999: Kargil War
Pakistani and Indian forces clash over Kashmir. Although it suffers heavy casualties, India wins the war.

LAC vs LoC

Often, when addressing border conflicts with Pakistan, we refer to the Line of Control (LoC). This is a ceasefire line negotiated by the UN at the end of the first Indo-Pak war in 1948. It is delineated on a map and internationally recognized. However, the Line of Actual Control (LAC) that comes up during border disputes featuring China is not agreed upon by either country. It is essentially a matter of perception and is neither delineated on a map nor demarcated on the ground.

PART 2

SEEDS OF DEVELOPMENT

7

Nuclear Age

On 16 July 1945, in the midst of the Second World War, US President Harry S. Truman wrote in his diary, 'We have discovered the most terrible bomb in the history of the world.' That day, at a desert in New Mexico, American scientists led by Robert Oppenheimer had tested the world's first nuclear bomb.

During the war, on 7 December 1941, Japan had launched a surprise attack on Pearl Harbour, a naval base of the US in Hawaii. Hundreds of aircraft were destroyed, several warships were wrecked and more than 2000 Americans died. An angry US retaliated fiercely. By March 1945, its air raids were wreaking havoc on Japan and in August, two nuclear bombs, code-named 'Little Boy' and 'Fat Man' were dropped on the Japanese cities of Hiroshima and Nagasaki.

Mushroom cloud

The explosions flattened large areas of land and caused raging firestorms that vapourized everything on the ground. Few living things—humans, plants or animals—survived to tell the tale. Monstrous mushroom clouds swirled high into the air. They were so huge that they could be seen from space. The bombings ended the Second World War, but they pushed the world into a dark and terrifying nuclear age, marked by the fear of nuclear weapons.

What is Nuclear Energy?

All chemical elements are made up of atoms. Inside each atom is a nucleus that holds large amounts of energy. This is known as atomic or nuclear energy. In most elements, nuclear energy remains contained within the nucleus. However, in radioactive elements like uranium and plutonium, the nucleus can be split to release this energy, which is so powerful that it can destroy anything that comes in its way.

Although free India was born in this violent age, non-violence had defined its freedom struggle. In keeping with this peaceful tradition, it shunned nuclear weapons and chose to pursue peaceful uses of nuclear energy. In the words of Jawaharlal Nehru:

> *'. . . we cannot help associating atomic energy with war. That is the present context of our lives. Nevertheless, the important thing today is that atomic energy is a*

vast source of power that is coming to the world . . . if we are to remain . . . a nation which keeps ahead of things, we must develop this atomic energy quite apart from war . . . we must develop it for . . . peaceful purposes.'

Atoms for Peace

Nuclear energy was identified with the most dreadful weapon of the times, but as scientists noted, it could be put to many good uses too—especially as a source of electricity. Most power plants in the world generate electricity by burning up fossil fuels such as coal and oil to boil water. Steam from the boiling water is used to turn turbines—large, wheel-shaped structures—that produce electricity. The release of nuclear energy also generates large amounts of heat—what if this heat was used to boil the water and release steam? Scientists agreed that this was a very good idea indeed. Not only are radioactive elements that release nuclear energy more abundantly available than fossil fuels, but nuclear energy is also far cleaner than the energy released by burning fossil fuels. It neither pollutes the air with smoke nor does it release greenhouse gases that make the world warmer and lead to climate change.

By the 1950s, countries around the world were promoting peaceful uses of nuclear energy. On 8 December 1953, the US President Dwight D. Eisenhower delivered a famous speech, 'Atoms for Peace', in which he urged the world to harvest the power of nuclear energy for peaceful uses. Following his speech, the US launched the Atoms for Peace programme that supplied equipment and information for peaceful nuclear research throughout the world. Meanwhile, after testing its first nuclear bomb in 1949, the USSR built the world's first fully-operational nuclear power plant at Obninsk in 1954.

Under the leadership of Nehru and the eminent nuclear scientist Homi Bhabha, newly independent India was also spending large amounts of money on pursuing peaceful uses of nuclear energy. In 1954, an atomic research centre was set up at Trombay near Bombay, which came to be called the Bhabha Atomic Research Centre (BARC) after Bhabha's death in 1966. With the help of countries around the world, scientists and engineers at BARC began developing India's first nuclear reactors. India also managed to acquire a powerful nuclear reactor from Canada, called CIRUS (Canada-India Reactor, US), for which the US had supplied heavy water, a form of water with radioactive properties. By 1969, the first nuclear power plant at Tarapur, near Bombay, was ready to begin operations.

Homi Bhabha and the Atomic Research Centre at Trombay

What is a nuclear reactor?

A nuclear reactor is a type of equipment that helps to release nuclear energy from radioactive elements.

Mounting Worries

Even as the world was promoting the peaceful use of nuclear energy, it was assailed by one big worry. The nuclear reactors that were being used to produce electricity could also be used to process nuclear fuel for weapons! In order to prevent such a situation, an international effort was made to establish safeguards. In 1957, the International Atomic Energy Agency (IAEA) was set up to monitor the use of nuclear technology and ensure that it was not being misused. A few years later, in 1963, over 120 countries around the world, including India, signed the Partial Test Ban Treaty (PTBT) that prohibited the testing of nuclear weapons in the atmosphere, in outer space and under water.

Yet, these measures were not able to adequately control the spread of nuclear weapons. By the beginning of the 1960s, literature on nuclear science had become widely available to the public and nuclear technology was not just being pursued by governments but also by private companies in a few countries. Plutonium, which powered nuclear weapons, was becoming easier to obtain. Hundreds of nuclear tests had been conducted, and in addition to the US and USSR, even the UK and France had declared themselves nuclear-weapon states. Calls for nuclear disarmament—

reducing or eliminating nuclear weapons—became strident. Safeguards were strengthened and in 1968, the Treaty on the Non-Proliferation of Nuclear Weapons, commonly known as the Non-Proliferation Treaty (NPT), was opened for signature. It banned the spread of nuclear weapons and their technology.

Alarm Bells for India

The world was becoming an increasingly insecure place. Alarm bells were set off in India when China successfully tested a nuclear weapon in 1964 and became the fifth nuclear-weapon state. Two years earlier, India had suffered a massive loss in a war against China and now it faced a very real nuclear threat. Feeling deeply concerned about its security, India approached other nuclear-weapon states requesting their protection if it was threatened. However, it failed to get sufficient support from them. Meanwhile, China continued testing more nuclear weapons.

In the midst of this turmoil, India rejected the NPT. It felt that treaties like the NPT were unfair because they stopped non-nuclear-weapon states from developing nuclear weapons and risked their safety by putting them at a disadvantage against countries that had already developed these weapons. For India, having a nuclear weapon was essential protection against security risks. So, towards the end of the 1960s, a group of scientists and engineers at BARC began serious work on developing nuclear weapons.

Smiling Buddha

After a series of endless struggles, doubts and worries, on the morning of 18 May 1974, the team at BARC tested India's first nuclear bomb at Pokhran, in Rajasthan. The desert trembled and Raja Ramanna, who led the team, conveyed the successful testing to Prime Minister Indira Gandhi with a coded message, 'The Buddha is smiling'. That's how the test, officially called Pokhran I, came to be known as 'Smiling Buddha'.

The government called it a 'peaceful nuclear explosion' and did not proclaim India as a nuclear-weapon state. Speaking to the media, Indira Gandhi said, *'This is our normal research and study . . . we are firmly committed to only peaceful uses of atomic energy.'* Despite this, India was jubilant—it finally had a nuclear bomb. But the rest of the world was startled. It questioned the power of the bomb India had tested. Many countries refused to believe India's 'peaceful' intentions. In 1975, some of them got together to form the Nuclear Suppliers Group (NSG), which stopped the export of nuclear technology and fuel to India. These included countries like Canada, the US and the UK that had helped India with its nuclear programme during the 1950s.

Panic in Pakistan

The NSG was a major setback for India. Even though it had tested a bomb, its nuclear programme was far from self-reliant and without necessary international help, it suffered.

But this was not the only fallout of Pokhran I. The test also led to panic in Pakistan, which had fought three wars against India and had suffered a major loss in the 1971 war. So, shortly after the test, Pakistan initiated its own nuclear weapons programme. Over the next two decades, tensions surged between the countries as each sought to boost its military might amid various economic and political challenges.

By the 1980s, Pakistan had made significant progress in its nuclear weapons programme. India grew worried and in 1983 it began to work on missiles that could fire nuclear explosives. This led to the development of missiles like 'Prithvi' and 'Agni' that are an important part of India's military armour. In response, Pakistan also began to develop such missiles.

Missile Man

An aeronautical engineer, A.P.J. Abdul Kalam helped India produce a number of successful missiles, including 'Agni', which earned him the nickname 'Missile Man'. He also played a prominent role in the 1998 nuclear tests and served as the President of India from 2002 to 2007.

The Desert Rumbles Again

Since Pokhran I, India had faced growing international pressure against its nuclear programme. Countries around the world wanted it to sign the NPT, but it refused to do this and struck out defiantly. Even as India was getting isolated internationally for continuing its nuclear programme, calls to boost nuclear might gathered momentum within the country. Scientists too were pressing the government to allow them to test the nuclear technology they had been developing.

On 6 April 1998, Pakistan tested 'Ghauri', a powerful missile that could cover close to 1500 km—which meant that unlike earlier missiles, it could be used to attack most of India's major cities. Feeling extremely uneasy about its security, India decided to take a bold step.

The very next month, on 11 May, the desert in Pokhran rumbled again. India detonated three nuclear bombs and declared itself a nuclear-weapon state. Two days later, on 13 May, it conducted two more tests. The world was shocked. The top-secret tests had come as a surprise. Still, India reiterated its peaceful intentions. On 18 May, Prime Minister Atal Bihari Vajpayee said, '*Our mindset is not in favour of a war. We wanted a nuclear deterrent. We conducted the tests.*' But few were convinced. Not to be outdone, on 28 May, Pakistan tested five nuclear bombs and two days later, on 30 May, it tested one more. On national television, Pakistan's Prime Minister Nawaz Sharif declared that the country had 'settled a score'.

In 1999, shortly after they had declared themselves nuclear-weapon states, India and Pakistan fought yet another war over Kashmir. The world was on an edge, over the possible use of nuclear weapons. Even though the war ended within three months and didn't involve nuclear weapons, it reminded the global community of the ever-present threat posed by such weapons, regardless of all peace initiatives.

So, Is Nuclear Energy Bad?

No one can deny the danger posed by the military use of nuclear energy. But in a rapidly developing world, the thirst for electricity can be just as overpowering. Nuclear energy has long been identified as a useful source of electricity. However, exposure to nuclear energy can be deadly for all living things. It can cause fatal diseases like cancer. Moreover, once this energy leaks into the environment, it can remain active for hundreds of years, prolonging the danger. In the years following the bombings at Hiroshima and Nagasaki, countless people died of sickness. This realization has only been aggravated by devastating accidents at nuclear power plants, prompting anti-nuclear protests around the world. In India, one of the most famous protests has been against the Kudankulam Nuclear Power Plant, close to the sea coast in Tamil Nadu. Local fishing communities have been worried that an accident at the plant could destroy their lives, poison the sea and endanger their livelihood. These protests grew even more forceful in 2011, when a tsunami led to a horrific meltdown at the Fukushima Daiichi Nuclear Power Plant along the sea coast in Japan. The accident had raised fears by triggering memories of the tsunami that had ravaged Tamil Nadu's coastline in 2004.

The protests prompted India to take a serious look at the safety concerns posed by nuclear energy. In 2011, it passed a nuclear liability law that defined who should be held responsible in case an accident took place and the ways in which they would be penalized. Nevertheless, the country continues its pursuit of peaceful nuclear power.

In 2008, it had closed a civil nuclear deal with the US that lifted the barriers imposed on it by the NSG in exchange for inspections by the IAEA to ensure the peaceful use of nuclear technology and fuel. Despite this push, nuclear energy contributes less than 4 per cent of India's electricity today. Many nuclear power plants, including the one at Kudankulam, have been plagued by operational problems. Apart from accidents, safety concerns have also been raised over mining radioactive elements for fuelling nuclear power and handling the radioactive waste produced by the power plants. Clearly, the dilemmas of the nuclear age are endless and it remains to be seen how India, like the rest of the world, copes with these.

Anti-nuclear protests at Kudankulam, Tamil Nadu

8

Rocketing into Space

On 4 October 1957, a loud beeping sound was heard around the world. It was coming all the way from space. The USSR had kicked off the space age by sending the first man-made satellite, Sputnik 1, into Earth's orbit. A few years later, in April 1961, Russian astronaut Yuri Gagarin became the first human to travel to space. Shortly afterwards, the eminent Indian scientist and industrialist Vikram Sarabhai proposed a space programme to the Indian government.

At the time, it would have been easy to laugh off his outrageous vision of how a developing nation like India could benefit from venturing into space. After all, space programmes are phenomenally expensive and newly independent India was a country with meagre means. But Prime Minister Jawaharlal Nehru was convinced that science and technology held the key to modernizing developing countries. Homi Bhabha, one of India's most influential scientists, who was also heading its nuclear programme, agreed that the country needed to pursue space research. So, in February 1962, India established the Indian National Committee for Space Research (INCOSPAR), and Sarabhai was appointed to lead it. His inspired leadership made Sarabhai the Father of India's space programme.

1. Rocket carrying a satellite, launched from Earth

2. Rocket begins to travel along Earth's orbit in space and releases satellite

3.Satellite begins to orbit the Earth

4. Satellite sends and receives signals to and from stations on Earth

Humble Beginnings

The ability to build and launch rockets is the foundation of all space programmes. After all, rockets are the vehicles that have transported humans and human engineering to space. INCOSPAR registered its humble beginning into the space age by deciding to launch a sounding rocket that would travel between 50 and 100 km above Earth and study the atmosphere.

Rockets take off with a powerful blast and sometimes instead of shooting upwards, they can unexpectedly change direction. This makes rocket launches a risky undertaking. To mitigate such risks, launch sites are typically located on remote and thinly populated coastal places. With a coastline of over 7000 km, India had several options open to it. In the end it chose Thumba, a tiny fishing hamlet along coastal Kerala that was situated on Earth's magnetic equator—an imaginary line over which one can find a flowing electric current called the Equatorial Electrojet (EEJ). The sounding rocket was going to study the EEJ in the atmosphere.

The local bishop and the people of Thumba generously made room for this grand undertaking despite the inconvenience it caused. Many of them had to shift to another village nearby. Their church—the heart of their small community—was acquired by INCOSPAR. The bishop's home was converted into an office and the church into a workshop, while cattle sheds served as storage houses and laboratories. The funding and facilities were scant. Many young scientists on the small team had no experience in space research. But what they lacked in experience, they more than made up with enthusiasm as they began assembling their very first rocket.

On 21 November 1963, India was ready for the launch. In the absence of other suitable transport, bicycles and bullock carts were used to carry parts of the rocket to the launch site—making for some truly iconic photographs! Local residents, political leaders, scientists, journalists . . . hundreds of people gathered to witness the spectacle. After a few anxious moments of waiting, the rocket finally took off at 6.25 p.m. The launch was an undisputed success.

Vikram Sarabhai and the rocket launch from Thumba

With barely any infrastructure and qualified people, India's first foray into space had relied heavily on international help. The mission was sponsored by the UN, the rocket had come from the US, the measuring instrument carried by it had come from France and the computer monitoring the mission had been supplied by the USSR. Sarabhai not only recruited Indian scientists and engineers working overseas into the space programme, he also sent local scientists and engineers to work overseas and gain experience and knowledge in space research. Long before it looked possible, he had dreamed of making India self-sufficient in space technology. It was this seemingly impossible dream that propelled the new-found space programme to work with ambition and overcome all odds.

Growing Aspirations

In April 1971, India received a letter from the Russian Academy of Sciences, offering to assist its space programme. The USSR agreed to launch an Indian satellite for free—but the satellite had to be built by India and completed by 1974, in time for the launch. This was massive task. India had practically no experience in building a satellite and to meet the deadline, it had to finish making one in less than three years. Opinion was divided. Some scientists thought this was an impossible task to pull off and wanted to pass up the offer. But it was finally decided that a free launch was too good an assistance to give up for a space programme that was just about finding its feet and had a long way to go.

The team worked round the clock to build a satellite that would study sunrays and conditions in the Earth's ionosphere (where the atmosphere meets space). They figured out some things on their own and for others, they reached out to other countries for help. The satellite was named 'Aryabhata' after the Indian mathematician and astronomer credited with introducing the concept of zero. On 19 April 1975, 'Aryabhata' was launched into space from the USSR. Thirty minutes later, the first signals were detected in India. Even though its electrical power supply eventually failed and several instruments could not work, it did return some data and survived well past the target of six months in space. It gave India the confidence to design, build and operate more satellites. In the decades following its launch, the Indian Space Research Organisation (ISRO)—formerly known as INCOSPAR—developed one of the largest national programmes of operational satellites that gather and transmit various kinds of information back to Earth.

The Wonders of Satellites

From the outset, India's space programme aspired to help the country's social and economic advancement. One of its earliest endeavours was the Satellite Instructional Television

Experiment (SITE) that was initiated in the 1970s. It utilised India's bare-bones space infrastructure at the time to set up a connection with an American communication satellite placed 36,000 km above Earth that helped broadcast educational TV programmes to community TV sets in 5000 villages across six Indian states, for a year. Despite several challenges, including unavailability of electricity or TV sets that did not work, SITE worked well enough for India to realize the value of satellites to meet a variety of development goals.

Viewers, who had no access to TV or cinema before, were hooked to the broadcast. Farmers reported that agricultural programmes had helped them understand new practices and the right kind and quantity of fertilizers to be used. Programmes on smallpox created awareness on the need for vaccination. The experiment also introduced social change by providing an avenue where people gathered to enjoy themselves and learn regardless of social differences such as gender and caste.

Since then, India's satellite programme has expanded exponentially. Today, it's easy to spot dish antennae poking out of rooftops. They catch satellite signals that transmit countless channels from all over the country and around the world into Indian homes. Apart from TV broadcasts, communication satellites that transmit information at high speeds are also used in various other telephone, mobile, radio and internet applications.

High mountains, hot deserts, cool coastlines, lush forests . . . India has one of the most geographically diverse landscapes. Have you ever wondered how it manages to keep track of such a vast expanse? Through satellites, of course! A multitude of earth observation or remote sensing satellites have helped India to map, monitor and manage its tremendous natural resources since the 1980s. Such information is particularly useful for people who depend directly on natural resources for their livelihood, such as farmers and fishermen. For example, it can inform farmers about the availability of groundwater in their land and help them locate the best place to dig a well. Similarly, it can tell fishermen when and where they should go fishing to get the best catch. Remote sensing data has also been of tremendous help in weather forecasting and disaster management. It has helped save countless lives by providing advance warnings of natural disasters such as cyclones and earthquakes.

Imagine you are lost in an unknown place and there is no one you can ask for directions. How would you find your way? If you have a device such as a mobile phone, you could possibly switch on the GPS (Global Positioning System), a network of satellites that transmit navigation data to devices on Earth. It will pick up your location and guide you to your destination. The GPS service was devised in the US during the 1960s and covers most of the globe today. In 2006, the Indian government approved a regional navigation satellite system that exclusively covers India. The first satellite under this was launched in 2013.

Becoming Self-sufficient

Simply building satellites—no matter how advanced—was never going to be enough. India had to be able to launch them too. Since rockets, or launch vehicles, are the only means to carry and place satellites in space, ISRO's first goal after the launch at Thumba, was to develop its own rockets. This was a formidable technological challenge that became even more complex when satellites had to be placed at higher orbits or weighed more.

In 1979, India was ready with its first rocket called SLV-3 (Satellite Launch Vehicle). But the test bombed, and the rocket was lost minutes after it took off from the launch pad. The scientists were deeply dejected. Years of hard work and crores of rupees had been riding on the test. But dejection would not do. So, they began again and the very next year India launched its satellite called Rohini, successfully into space. With this, it became the sixth nation in the world to be able to design, build and launch its own satellites.

The SLV rockets were able to carry spacecraft weighing up to 40 kg into Low Earth Orbit that extends a few thousand kilometres above Earth and is closest to it. Gradually, ISRO developed rockets that were able to carry heavier spacecraft and place them on higher orbits. Its greatest success so far came in the form of the Polar Satellite Launch Vehicle (PSLV) that was first tested successfully in October 1994. In the years since then, it has grown to become ISRO's most trusted launch vehicle. The PSLV has been used to launch a majority of India's most important satellites as well as the Chandrayaan and Mangalyaan missions that carried spacecraft to the Moon and to Mars. Even though India continues to develop its launch capabilities, with the PSLV it came closest to realizing Sarabhai's dream of self-sufficiency in space technology.

With increasing self-sufficiency came an incredible opportunity. India was now in a position to earn money through its space programme by assisting other countries and companies with space technology. In September 1992, the Government of India established Antrix (an anglicized version of the Sanskrit word 'Antariksh', meaning space or sky), a company that would negotiate commercial space agreements for ISRO, with national and international clients. Since then, India has provided services such as space launches and data from its satellites to various clients.

ISRO Rockets (L-R): SLV, ASLV, PSLV, GSLV and GSLV III

An Indian in Space

Sarabhai may have marvelled at Yuri Gagarin's trip into space, but he had no such ambitions for India. The technology for Human Spaceflight (HSF) was much too advanced, risky and prohibitively expensive for a developing nation. So, in 1980, when Prime Minister Indira Gandhi approached ISRO with an offer from the USSR to send an Indian astronaut on an eight-day trip to space, the organization declined. HSF did not feature in its plans at the time and it was unwilling to devote resources for this. The next best place to find astronauts was the Indian Air Force (IAF). So, the Prime Minister approached it and the IAF agreed.

Around 200 IAF pilots volunteered for the programme. Shortlisted candidates were only informed of the true nature of the mission when they had to undergo intensive medical tests. On 3 April 1984, after eighteen months of training, Wing Commander Rakesh Sharma became the first Indian to travel to space aboard a Soviet spacecraft called Soyuz T-11. With him, were the Soviet astronauts Yuri Malyshev and Gennady Strekalov. As the only member of the crew with no previous experience of spaceflight, Sharma's main role was to monitor instruments and conduct experiments. One of his experiments involved performing yoga in space! A highlight of his trip was the brief conversation he had with Indira Gandhi. When she asked him how India looked from space, he famously remarked '*Saare Jahan Se Accha*' (best in the world), quoting the lyrics of a famous Hindi song. This exchange was broadcast on national television and led to a media flurry. India was enthralled, but in the absence of a formal plan for HSF, Sharma's trip remained an exception.

Rakesh Sharma (centre) with the Soviet astronauts Gennady Strekalov (L) and Yuri Malyshev (R)

Shortly after his return, two Indian candidates travelled to the US to undergo further tests for another HSF mission planned by the US space agency, National Aeronautics and Space Administration (NASA). But it was called off after the horrific explosion of the space shuttle Challenger on 28 January 1986, which claimed the lives of seven astronauts and sent shockwaves through NASA. Yet, HSF remains a natural aspiration for space programmes around the world and its allure has been hard to resist. Currently, ISRO too is preparing to launch an Indian crew into space under its Gaganyaan programme—formally announced in 2018.

Space Defence

Over the years, India's space programme has been widely acknowledged for achieving remarkable feats. One of its most celebrated achievements came on 24 September 2014 when its Mars Orbiter Mission (Mangalyaan) entered the orbit of the red planet about 300 days after leaving Earth. It was a historic moment—India had become the first nation to reach Mars in its very first attempt and it had accomplished this on an unbelievably economical budget. The hugely popular mission was even adapted into books, films and TV shows. But in 2019, India's space programme hit news headlines for a very different reason. It had alarmed the world by successfully conducting an anti-satellite missile test.

One of the most debatable uses of satellites lies in the field of defence. A satellite in space can pick up sensitive information that could aid as well as compromise a nation's security. Intelligence-gathering or spy satellites can survey pre-selected areas to transmit extremely detailed images of what is happening on the ground. During a war, having such satellites can provide key information on enemy locations to a country's army and help it launch an effective attack. However, spy satellites also pose a grave security risk because they can leak a country's top-secret missions to its opponents. Following the Kargil war in 1999, India began to grow its capability in spy satellites in order to protect its borders. But to truly counter the threat posed by these satellites, it needed to develop an anti-satellite system that could destroy such satellites. This need became even more urgent after China successfully tested an anti-satellite missile in 2007. Having suffered a massive defeat in the 1962 war against China, India was determined to do everything in its power to ensure its safety.

The ability to destroy a satellite orbiting in space is an enormous military feat since it involves targeting a fast-moving object with a moving weapon. The chances of error are very high. When India successfully accomplished this in 2019, it became the fourth nation after the US, USSR and China to possess an anti-satellite missile. Although Sarabhai's original vision was to keep India's space programme away from military uses, growing security threats in its neighbourhood made this inevitable.

Space junk

If you ever get to travel to space, one of the first things you're likely to encounter is a vast mass of floating space junk. Inactive satellites and broken pieces of satellites make up a bulk of it.

A Much-feted Programme

India's space programme has come a very long way from its humble beginning in Thumba. It has grown from strength to strength, winning worldwide acclaim. Inspired by its remarkable success, various private start-ups have been tinkering with space technology since the 2000s. Students in schools and colleges have been participating in various national and international space science contests. What once seemed like an outrageous adventure has today grown into a stunning spectacle of India's technological might in one of the most advanced forms of human endeavour.

India in Space

1962: INCOSPAR formed under the Department of Atomic Energy (DAE), renamed ISRO in 1969

1963: First sounding rocket launched from Thumba

1965: Space Science and Technology Centre, now called the Vikram Sarabhai Space Centre, established in Thumba

1967: First Earth Station—ground infrastructure required to connect Earth to satellites in space—opens in Ahmedabad

1971: Vikram Sarabhai dies; first spaceport—Satish Dhawan Space Centre—established in Sriharikota, Andhra Pradesh

Aryabhata: India's first satellite

1972: Government establishes a dedicated Department of Space (DoS); ISRO shifts from DAE to DoS; ISRO Satellite Centre, now called the UR Rao Satellite Centre, established in Bangalore (now Bengaluru).

1975: First indigenous satellite Aryabhata launched from the USSR; Satellite Instructional Television Experiment launched

1979: First experimental remote sensing satellite, Bhaskara-1, launched by the USSR

1980: India becomes the 6th nation in the world to be able to design, build and launch satellites, after its Satellite Launch Vehicle (SLV 3) successfully places the satellite Rohini 1 into space

1981: India's first experimental communication satellite, Ariane Passenger PayLoad Experiment (APPLE), launched by the European Space Agency

1982: First multipurpose communication and meteorology satellite INSAT-1 launched by NASA

1983: Rakesh Sharma becomes the first Indian to travel to space

1988: First operational remote sensing satellite launched by the USSR

1992: India builds its launch capabilities by successfully testing the Augmented Satellite Launch Vehicle (ASLV); Government of India establishes Antrix Corporation, a company that would negotiate commercial space agreements for ISRO

1994: India expands its launch capabilities by successfully testing its PSLV

1999: First foreign satellites, from South Korea and Germany, launched by the PSLV

2001: India continues to build its launch capabilities by successfully testing the Geosynchronous Satellite Launch Vehicle (GSLV), Technology Experiment Satellite launched by the PSLV becomes a prototype for future spy satellites

2004: First communication satellite dedicated to education—EDUSAT—launched by the GSLV

2005: First remote sensing satellite—CARTOSAT-1—launched by the PSLV

2008: Chandayaan-1, India's first moon mission launched by the PSLV, reaches the moon

2013: India's first satellite dedicated to military use launched by the European Space Agency; first navigation satellite launched by the PSLV

2014: Mangalyaan, India's first mars mission launched by the PSLV, reaches Mars

2015: First satellite dedicated to astronomy—AstroSat—launched by the PSLV

2016: India begins testing a reusable launch vehicle (currently, launch vehicles cannot be used for more than one launch).

2017: India breaks a space record by successfully launching 104 satellites together

2018: India announces Gaganyaan—the first mission to carry an Indian crew into space

2019: India becomes the fourth country in the world to possess anti-satellite technology

9

Fighting Hunger

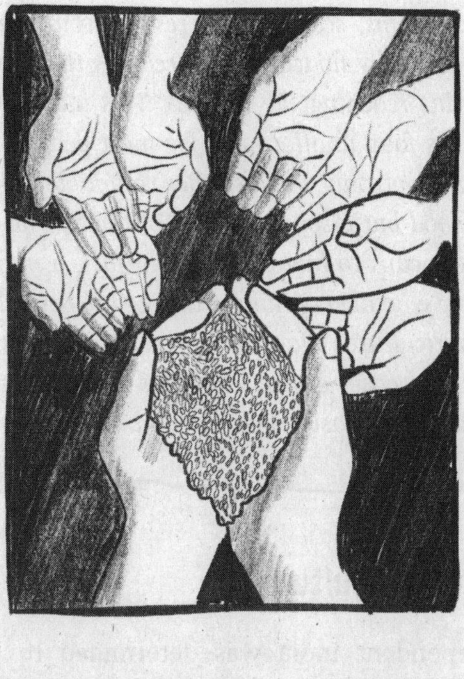

In 1943, nearly 30 lakh people died of hunger in Bengal as large quantities of food grains were hoarded and shipped off to British soldiers, fighting in the Second World War. The price of available food skyrocketed and most people were unable to afford even a morsel. Scenes of mass starvation shocked the country and made the battle against hunger its most pressing concern.

What makes a nation go hungry?

Nations get a bulk of their food from agriculture. It's easy to think that if agriculture produces enough food, there won't be any scarcity and people will be well fed. But this is not always the case. While poor agricultural produce, owing to reasons such as undeveloped agriculture, unfavourable weather, pest attacks, etc., certainly causes problems, scarcity also results from man-made causes, especially hoarding that reduces the quantity of food grains reaching the market. This increases prices and makes food unaffordable for most people. Nations go hungry not only because they're unable to produce enough food but also when most of their people do not have the means to buy this food. In fact, a majority of the people who died of hunger during the Bengal famine were agricultural labourers, fishermen, transport workers and other casual labourers who were too poor to afford the increasing price of food.

Prioritizing Agriculture

Newly independent India was determined to feed all its people. So, agriculture became one of its greatest priorities. Centuries of British rule had ruined India's agriculture by placing excessive power in the hands of upper-caste landlords. The main interest of the landlords was to collect rent from the farmers tilling their land, pay a share to the British and profit with the rest. They neither engaged in farming nor were they concerned about the problems of farmers. This left farmers in deep despair and crushed their productivity. Independent India wanted to address this historic injustice and boost agricultural productivity.

Large areas of forest land were cleared for agriculture and given to farmers. The government also invested heavily in big dams for irrigation and electricity generation like Bhakra-Nangal in Punjab, Damodar Valley in West Bengal and Hirakud in Orissa. Vinoba Bhave, a leading disciple of Mahatma Gandhi, toured the country, persuading landlords to donate their lands to farmers. He asked people in villages to pool their lands and own them jointly, and he requested city dwellers to contribute money and labour to uplift those less privileged than them. Meanwhile, the government abolished landlordism to make farmers the owners of land and free them from the burden of rent. In addition to this, it also wanted to implement 'land ceiling'—limits on the size of land an individual could own. Both these forms of land reform were bitterly opposed by landlords. Even though the government abolished landlordism, it was unable to implement the system of land ceiling that would have helped to free up even more land. In the end, the land reforms benefitted some farmers a lot more than others. Typically, the beneficiaries belonged to the more powerful intermediate castes, while those from the lower castes continued to work as landless labourers.

Battling Food Shortages

Cinema vans toured the country showing films that educated people on the food crisis. A strict system of rationing was put in place to manage the distribution of scarce food grains, control prices and prevent hoarding and wastage. Ration cards were distributed that allowed people to buy a fixed amount of food from government-supported ration shops, at economical prices. There were several restrictions on public events that involved a feast. National leaders urged people to cut down food consumption by going on fasts. But nothing seemed to work.

In some places, the system of rationing was abused by dishonest ration shop owners who profited by selling grains to hoarders and contaminating supplies with stones, chaff, bran, etc., making them unfit for consumption. Many people were so hungry that calls for fasting seemed almost unnecessary.

People queuing up at a ration shop in the initial decades after Independence

The acute shortage of wheat and rice prompted the government to advocate ways of reducing and replacing these grains in food menus! In 1949, Jawaharlal Nehru declared that he had quit rice and was eating rotis made with a mix of sweet potatoes and wheat. The government also distributed cookbooks with recipes that didn't use wheat and rice.

Green Revolution

By the 1960s, India's food crisis had become a nightmare. The country suffered back-to-back droughts, a famine was declared in Bihar, massive protests took place, against soaring food prices and food riots broke out in many places as hungry people looted grains. Vast quantities of food grains had to be imported to prevent mass-starvation. India signed one of the biggest deals with the US. Under this deal, it imported wheat that arrived on its shores in ships, before being distributed to people across the country. That's why India was said to be living a 'ship-to-mouth' existence. But buying so much food was expensive and India didn't have a lot of money. So, it was constantly worried about the expenses. Besides, being dependent on other countries for something as basic as food is never a good idea. What if they suddenly stopped supplies?

Despite all its efforts, the government had failed to provide enough food for the growing population. But the new minister for food and agriculture, Chidambaram Subramaniam, had some revolutionary ideas in mind. Born into a family of farmers, he went on to study science and law and emphasized the need to boost agricultural science in the pursuit of productivity.

Subramaniam improved the pay and working conditions of agricultural scientists. He encouraged different states to set up agricultural universities that would research local crops and began to zealously look into better-quality seeds that would yield a higher quantity of food crops. Beginning with his own lawns, Subramaniam set up several experimental fields where scientists could test new varieties of seeds. He was ably assisted in his ideas by Balaram Sivaraman, an eminent government official working with him, and M.S. Swaminathan, a gifted agricultural scientist.

In 1944, when India was still fighting for independence, thousands of kilometres away, at the International Maize and Wheat Improvement Centre in Mexico, scientists led by Norman Borlaug were experimenting with seeds that could boost food production. Eventually, they developed a variety of dwarf wheat that produced two to three times more grain than ordinary wheat. That's why these crops were called high-yielding varieties and they ushered a Green Revolution that changed the agricultural fortunes of Mexico. By 1964, the country that once imported half its wheat was producing enough to export five lakh tonnes! This was exactly the sort of 'miracle' Subramaniam was seeking in India. With his backing, Swaminathan began directing research teams to adapt the Mexican variety of high-yielding wheat to Indian conditions and went on to father the Green Revolution in India.

Field demonstration with M.S. Swaminathan (centre) and Norman Borlaug (R) as a farmer and some officials look on.

By the mid-1960s, demonstrations were being held on experimental fields to show India the wonders of the new scientifically engineered seeds, and promotions were made through national media, such as newspapers and All India Radio. Names of the new seed varieties were being whispered among farmers across the country. The Green Revolution had arrived in India, along with a whole new way of farming.

New Ways of Farming

Before the Green Revolution farmers would usually grow local varieties of crops that were best suited to the soil and climate in the area. Seeds were saved during each harvest and sown again. They were cultivated using old-fashioned wooden ploughs, waterwheels, bullock carts and organic manure. Sources of irrigation were underdeveloped and most farmers relied on rainfall. However, this age-old way of farming did not suit the high-yielding varieties.

Farmers had to buy new seeds every sowing season. The yield would not be the same if they saved and re-sowed seeds from the old harvest. They had to invest in modern farming that involved adequate irrigation, chemical fertilizers and pesticides, and advanced farming equipment, such as tractors. All this required huge amounts of money. To overcome this challenge, the Green Revolution was initially introduced in states that had a relatively prosperous class of farmers who owned large tracts of well-irrigated land, like Punjab. The government offered a variety of benefits (subsidies and incentives) to farmers to encourage the adoption of the new seeds. It reduced the cost of fertilizers and electricity to pump out groundwater for irrigation. The farmers were guaranteed a pre-decided Minimum Support Price (MSP) at which their produce would be procured. These grains were purchased by a body called the Food Corporation of India and made available for public distribution through ration shops and other food schemes launched by the government.

The allure of this enticing new agricultural package and the plentiful yield was hard to resist. By the 1970s, Indian agriculture had been transformed and the country was finally producing enough food grains to feed all its people.

Unsustainable Changes

Although the Green Revolution helped solve the problem of famines, the changes it introduced in farming eventually became difficult to sustain. Indiscriminate use of water, chemical pesticides and fertilizers degraded the land and polluted the natural environment. By the 1980s, many farmers found that the natural fertility of the soil had reduced and it needed a larger dose of chemical fertilizers. Pests had become immune to pesticides and crop diseases were destroying yields. Groundwater levels had fallen and they needed to dig deeper and deeper to pump out sufficient water. Crop yields were beginning to fall, but the cost of growing them was only increasing as farmers kept having to buy seeds and invest in more fertilizers, pesticides, agricultural equipment and irrigation facilities. They became overly reliant on government support and many of them ended up borrowing so much money for farming that they fell into a cycle of debt. The ecological crisis not only hit agricultural productivity but also worsened public health.

The popularity of the high-yielding varieties and the government support for them meant that more and more farmers filled their fields with these crops. Over time, wheat and rice displaced other food crops, such as nutritious pulses, reducing crop diversity. Without crop diversity, our food menus would remain limited, our nutritional needs might not be met and we might not have sufficient replacements if popular crops begin to fail owing to worsening climatic conditions, pests and diseases.

>60 per cent

of the total crop production worldwide is dominated by nine crops: sugar cane, maize, rice, wheat, potatoes, soybeans, oil-palm, sugar beet, cassava (FAO, 2014)

Agricultural Inequality

The Green Revolution made farming much more expensive. Even though it led to bumper yields and increased agricultural income, these benefits were largely cornered by rich farmers from intermediate castes, who could afford the expenses. Over time, economic inequality in rural India worsened as rich farmers became even richer, while the poor continued to suffer. The introduction of machines like tractors reduced the need for manual labour in farming, which further hurt the livelihood of landless labourers.

As the economic might of rich farmers increased, many of them became extremely popular. Despite the glaring inequalities, they came to be seen as representatives of rural India and gained a large following among farming communities. This gave them political power, as they were able to draw in a large number of rural voters, win elections and influence government decisions that impacted agriculture. Massive peasant rallies and protests became increasingly common as farmers became more vocal about their needs and problems. As recently as 2021, the government had to withdraw three agricultural laws it had been proposing after a year-long protest by farmers.

In 1979, Chaudhary Charan Singh became the first farm leader to be sworn in as India's Prime Minister.

In the decades following the Green Revolution, farmer protests and rallies became increasingly common.

Food Insecurity

Today, it is claimed that if all the grain sacks in India were laid out in a row, they would reach the moon and back! The desperate food shortage that plagued the country in the early decades is over. Despite this, crores of poor people, especially children, remain hungry. They either don't get enough to eat or the food they eat isn't nutritious enough. Due to these problems, many children are either too short for their age, weigh too little, or both. They're so weak that many of them die before they are five years old. This happens because even though India is producing enough food, it hasn't been as successful in ensuring that everyone has access to this food and is able to afford it. Lack of access to affordable and nutritious food is called food insecurity.

Over the years, India has made various attempts to overcome food insecurity. The Midday Meal Scheme—a scheme to offer nutritious meals in schools—that began in Tamil Nadu in the 1960s has been implemented across different states. In 2013, the Parliament also passed a National Food Security Act, which made a large population of poor people eligible for 5 kg of cheaply priced cereals every month. Employment schemes in poor areas have helped to increase purchasing power among the needy while expansion of the national road network has helped to transport grains to scarcity areas. Despite such measures, a large population of the country struggles to get two square meals a day.

It is estimated that by 2050, India's population would touch 160 crore. To effectively fight hunger, India not only needs to produce enough food it also needs to enhance storage, transportation, distribution and affordability to ensure that the food it is producing reaches all its people and nourishes them.

10

A Billion-Litre Idea

In the 1970s, five lakh dairy farmers gave two rupees each to produce the movie *Manthan*. It told everyone the story of how farmers had come together to transform Independent India from a milk-deficient country to one of the largest milk producers in the world. And what a blockbuster tale it was!

Milk Woes

Back in the 1960s, Indian cities were suffering from an acute milk crisis. Despite having one of the largest cattle populations in the world, India was importing vast quantities of milk powder to meet the needs of its people. This was happening because of the way milk was being supplied to the cities.

Milk was mainly produced in rural areas. In the absence of advanced dairy practices, neither were the cattle producing enough milk nor were the farmers able to preserve and transport it to cities. Instead, they were selling it to unscrupulous middlemen who in turn sold it to suppliers in cities. All the profits from the sale of the milk were cornered by the suppliers and the middlemen, while the farmers continued to be underpaid. This kept the dairy industry in rural areas largely underdeveloped and it was unable to keep up with the rising demand for milk in the cities.

To make up for the shortage, private vendors in the cities provided milk from their own sheds. Every year, the most high-yielding buffaloes were transported to these sheds as soon as they gave birth to a calf. The calves were also brought to induce the buffaloes to produce milk. Gradually, the buffaloes were trained to produce milk without the presence of their calves. Once the training was successful, the calves were sent off to slaughterhouses, as were the buffaloes who stopped producing milk. Not only was this practice extremely cruel, it was also slowly destroying the population of the most high-yielding buffaloes. Moreover, the conditions in these sheds were often so unhygienic that the animals were stressed and produced poor quality milk. But a group of dairy farmers and an inventive young man in the sleepy little town of Anand held a remarkable answer to this milk crisis.

Queue for milk outside a milk depot in the initial decades after Independence

During the 1970s, thirteen-year-old Rajiv would wake up at the crack of dawn—not to get ready for school, but to line up at the milk depot in his colony in Delhi. As the second eldest among his four brothers, he was entrusted with this responsibility twice every week. If he reached the depot after 6.30 a.m., the queue would become much too long, with nearly forty to fifty people awaiting their turn! Sometimes, standing in the queue became too much to bear and people temporarily left to sit down for a few moments—but not before they had marked their spot with a stone or rock. There was no question of asking anyone to save their spot. Milk was in such short supply that once the depot window opened, it was war! You either rushed and got your milk or you returned empty-handed. Getting just two litres of milk for a family of four brothers and their parents was a struggle. The quantity was barely enough, but milk was rationed and getting more was difficult. The deficit was either made up by using milk powder or by buying milk at astronomical prices from crooked doodhwalas *(milk vendors) who routinely diluted it with large amounts of impure water!*

Origins of the Milk Revolution

In the district of Kaira, situated close to Anand, a group of dairy farmers had got together to form the Kaira District Cooperative Milk Producers Union Limited (KDCMPUL) in the 1940s. They would pool all their milk, so they would have enough to not just sell it at a good price, but to also enjoy bargaining power over the buyers. Even though the government supported them, their action was a bold move for the times. They found themselves in a pitched battle with the private buyer who was supplying their milk to the city of Bombay. Eventually, the farmers took a daring step. Instead of supplying milk through the buyer, they decided to supply it themselves. No one believed that they could pull this off. After all, they didn't have any technical skills required for the milk business. But the farmers were determined. They leased part of an old dairy in Anand and began their work. However, the machines were so ancient that they frequently broke down and the farmers kept running into technical trouble, until they met a man who not only solved their problems but also gave wings to their bold initiative.

Verghese Kurien landed in Anand on 13 May 1949. The government had sent him to work in its research creamery there. It was the last thing he wanted to do. Kurien had a passion for metallurgy and nuclear physics. In fact, he had even studied these subjects in the US. But the government had funded his foreign education on the condition that once he returned, he would pursue dairy engineering. If he refused to follow these orders, he would have to return the 30,000 rupees that the government had spent on his education. Left with no option, Kurien reluctantly arrived in Anand. Used to living in big cities, he found life in the little town mighty boring. So, he began to look around for something to do in his free time. That's when he bumped into Tribhuvandas Patel, the leader of the dairy farmers. Patel had reached out to the young, foreign-educated dairy engineer to solve the technical trouble plaguing the KDCMPUL.

Kurien was shocked when he saw the outdated and dilapidated equipment the farmers were using to process their milk. Initially, he helped them repair it, but eventually he convinced them to replace it with modern machinery. In 1950, he officially joined KDCMPUL. He also roped in his friend, Harichand Dalaya, an expert in the methods and technologies of modern dairying. After that, there was no turning back for this revolution that changed the face of dairying in India.

(L-R) Verghese Kurien, Tribhuvandas Patel and Harichand Dalaya

Dairy animals do not produce the same quantity of liquid milk throughout the year. In some seasons they produce much more than in others. To cope with this fluctuation, dairies around the world turn excess milk into milk powder. When the animals produce less milk, the milk powder is turned back into milk to make up for the shortfall. But dairy farmers in India did not have the technology and skills to turn milk into milk powder. Moreover, unlike other countries, most milk in India came from buffaloes instead of cows—and no one had attempted to mass manufacture milk powder from buffalo milk. Kurien and Dalaya managed to pull off this feat and built a new dairy, with modern equipment donated by the UN, which manufactured milk powder from buffalo milk. For the first time in the history of India, dairy farmers owned the country's most technologically advanced dairy. KDCMPUL was now not only producing liquid milk but also milk powder. Soon, it began producing other milk products like butter, condensed milk, cheese and baby food under a new brand name—Anand Milk Union Limited (AMUL)—that became hugely popular.

The first advertisement featuring the iconic Amul girl with the caption 'Utterly Butterly Delicious' was displayed in Bombay in 1966.

Operation Flood

Everything about Anand, from its weather to its buffaloes, was ordinary. Then how was AMUL thriving in the 1960s and '70s, when almost all other dairies in India had failed and the country was facing a milk crisis? What was the secret behind its stupendous success? Prime Minister Lal Bahadur Shastri needed an answer and he turned to Kurien.

The answer was simple. Unlike the other dairies that were either owned by the government or by private vendors, AMUL was owned by dairy farmers. The farmers chose their leaders and their leaders hired professionals like Kurien to run the enterprise. When AMUL did well, the farmers benefitted the most. The Prime Minister was extremely excited. If the success of AMUL was not because of any special conditions prevailing in Anand, its model could be copied elsewhere too. So, he gave Kurien a free hand to take this 'Anand Model' all over India, giving birth to 'Operation Flood'—a billion-litre idea that would transform India's milk fortune.

Initiated in 1970, Operation Flood established a giant national milk grid that did away with middlemen and private vendors to directly connect milk producers with consumers in over 700 towns and cities across India. Large dairies were built in major cities like Delhi, Bombay, Calcutta and Madras. These dairies got their milk from cooperative dairying areas, known as milksheds, which followed the 'Anand Model' of empowering dairy farmers. The liquid milk would be transported by rail and road in special tankers that prevented it from getting spoilt. At the end of three decades, India had become one of the largest milk producers in the world.

Social Growth and Change

The dairy cooperatives at the heart of Operation Flood not only caused a milk revolution, but also brought a social revolution to India's villages. They broke down age-old social barriers of gender, caste and class. The queues at milk collection centres were strictly on a first come, first served basis. People could not demand any special treatment because of their caste or class. Similarly, the milk that was collected was treated in exactly the same way and no one stopped to inquire the social status or caste of the household it came from. The dairy farmers earned money only on the basis of the amount of milk they were able to contribute rather than the caste or class they belonged to. Women, who usually cared for and milked the cattle, played an active role in the cooperatives and began to earn greater income from the sale of the milk. Often, they ended up earning as much money as their husbands. This empowered them and increased their say in the way their families spent money.

Exposure to modern technology and techniques also influenced other aspects of village life. The dairies had to be kept clean to prevent milk from getting contaminated. This emphasis on cleanliness taught the farmers the importance of hygiene. Similarly, medical care of dairy animals by veterinarians and appropriate nutrition for them also inspired the farmers to seek better healthcare and nutrition for themselves. Many cooperatives ran successful healthcare programmes, especially for women and children.

Much like the Green Revolution the gains from the milk revolution were also unevenly distributed. Rich farmers who owned a larger number of cattle and were able to shelter and feed them well ended up contributing a bulk of the milk and earned more than others. Those belonging to states with larger urban areas and better road and rail facilities did even better. Nevertheless, the movement highlighted how extraordinary social growth and change could be achieved by placing ordinary people at the centre of development plans.

The milk revolution modernised dairy farming in India and empowered dairy farmers

Before

After

PART 3
TRYING TIMES

11

An Era of Protests

By the end of the 1960s, the colour of Independence had waned. Two major wars in 1962 and 1965 and acute food shortages caused by severe droughts had drained India's coffers and led to economic upheaval (*also see page 182*). Although India had been a democracy for more than two decades, voting and placing representatives in the government had not addressed many of its most pressing concerns. Poverty and scarcity were rampant and the masses were distraught. The government appeared to have failed them.

Giving a Verdict

In the elections held in 1967, the Congress party, which had been in power since Independence, suffered heavy losses for the first time. Even though it was still in majority, it got only 283 seats in the Lok Sabha, compared to 361 in the previous election. Non-Congress governments came to power in states like Madras (now Tamil Nadu) and Kerala. In others, like West Bengal and Orissa (now Odisha), it had to form coalition governments with other state parties. This era saw the rise of strong regional parties, such as the Dravida Munnetra

Kazhagam (DMK) in Tamil Nadu and stiff competition for the ruling Congress.

The people had given their verdict through their votes. But this wasn't the end of their protest. They had many grievances and left no stone unturned in an effort to ensure that the government heard what they had to say.

Different People, Different Causes

In a country as diverse as India, even the grievances had remarkable plurality. During the 1970s, many of them emerged as movements that gained momentum among different social groups in different parts of the country.

After the death of India's second Prime Minister Lal Bahadur Shastri, the Congress had instated forty-eight-year-old Indira Gandhi, the daughter of Jawaharlal Nehru, in his place. Even though India got its first woman Prime Minister, ordinary women across the country continued to suffer gender discrimination. They now began to raise their voice on issues of gender equality and violence against women.

Treated as 'untouchables' by India's caste-ridden society, Dalits had suffered centuries of oppression. Anguished by ceaseless atrocities, such as murders, assaults, lynching, land-grabbing and denial of land for cremating their dead, Dalit youth in the slums of Bombay (now Mumbai) initiated the Dalit Panther Movement (DPM), which advocated militancy and self-defence to combat such violence. The movement was inspired by B.R. Ambedkar and a political organization in the US called the Black Panthers, which challenged police brutality against African Americans. Since the founders of the DPM were poets and writers, they created a rich body of literature describing their struggles. In the poem 'Cruelty' (originally in Marathi), Namdeo Dhasal of the DPM wrote:

The living spirit looking out
of hundreds of thousands of sad, pitiful eyes
Has shaken me.
I am broken by the revolt exploding inside me.

In the Himalayan villages of Uttarakhand (then part of Uttar Pradesh), people were outraged when the government allowed large-scale industrial felling of their forests, but refused to give them the permission to fell a few trees for their small-scale enterprises and needs. So, men, women and children hugged their trees to protest and demand equal rights over the natural resources of the region. This was the Chipko Andolan that made global headlines and spurred similar movements in other parts of India and even overseas.

Peasants had long been protesting against unscrupulous landlords who evicted them from their lands and hoarded grain. However, at Naxalbari in West Bengal, this protest turned into a violent uprising. Peasant leaders took to arms. They clashed with the police and beheaded landlords. Even though the government in the state came down heavily upon them, they quickly achieved an iconic status. The term 'naxalite' came to stand for militant revolutionaries, fighting against those in power to secure the rights of the oppressed and dispossessed.

Impacting Political Fortunes

In an effort to console the protesting masses, Indira Gandhi proposed a ten-point programme of reform that attempted to address the problems of poverty and unemployment. Among other things, it advocated government control of banking, abolition of privileges granted to rulers of the princely states at the time of Independence and guaranteeing minimum wages for rural and industrial labour. However, senior leaders of the Congress felt that the reforms would exhaust administrative resources and refused to allow them.

Indira Gandhi was frustrated. No matter what she tried, her efforts were thwarted. Eventually, the difference in opinion grew too big and senior leaders expelled her from the Congress. The eighty-four-year-old party was ruptured, and Indira Gandhi walked out with her followers to form a new Congress (R) [Requisitionist]. She still had enough support and continued to remain Prime Minister. However, to push her reforms through, she needed greater political power. So, in 1970, she called for an election—fourteen months ahead of schedule.

The Lok Sabha was dissolved for the first time in the political history of the Independent India, and Indira Gandhi took to vigorous campaigning. She travelled close to 58,000 km in ten weeks, addressed hundreds of meetings and was heard or seen by crores of Indians. Her slogan 'Garibi Hatao' (Remove Poverty) resonated with the destitute masses and she won a spectacular victory, surpassing even her father's. The Congress that had been humiliated in the last election held in 1967, found new wings under her. With power firmly in her hands, Indira Gandhi began to implement her reforms and strengthen her hold over the government. India's decisive victory in the 1971 war against Pakistan only increased her popularity. 'Indira is India, India is Indira' became a popular slogan among her supporters.

Yet, the problems of poverty and scarcity remained unresolved. Rising reports of corruption in the government only increased people's frustration with the state of affairs in the country. Public anger boiled over, leading to a protest that came to define the decade.

Students Take to the Streets

College students of the time—the first generation of children born in Independent India—were among those most disillusioned by the problems around them. Corruption, unemployment, and food shortages made their future look bleak. Rebellion seemed like the only way out. This led to a movement that was born in college campuses but soon spread throughout different states. Strikes, blockades and instances of lawlessness became increasingly common and rattled the government.

In January 1974, college students in Gujarat began protesting against the notoriously corrupt government in their state. They demanded its dismissal. Soon, the protests turned violent. Angry students burned buses and government offices. The Chief Minister Chimanbhai Patel was forced to resign and Gujarat came under the control of the central government.

Called Nav Nirman or the movement for regeneration, the protests in Gujarat inspired a similar struggle in Bihar. On 18 March 1974, student groups encircled the state assembly in Patna. Clashes broke out between the protestors and the police. As news spread about the trouble in Patna, more clashes broke out in other parts of the state.

Soon afterwards, the students requested seventy-four-year-old Jayaprakash Narayan (JP) to lead their movement. A veteran politician and freedom fighter who had been part of several movements and worthy causes, JP was known for his integrity, and the students looked up to him. He agreed to their request and under him, the movement grew rapidly. On 5 June 1974, he led a massive procession through Patna and called for a 'total revolution' to rid India of all its problems.

The immense popularity of JP was hard to ignore. On 1 November 1974, the central government attempted to reconcile the protestors by offering to dissolve the state assembly in Bihar, provided the movement dropped its demand for dissolution of other state assemblies. But JP declined the offer. Three days later when he was manhandled by policemen in Patna, pictures of him warding off the policemen while stumbling to the ground were splashed across newspapers, sparking outrage.

In March 1975, the movement held one of the largest processions ever seen, in Delhi. About 7,50,000 participants streamed into the national capital. While most of them were students from Bihar and Uttar Pradesh, several others joined in. Many parties opposing the Congress also supported the movement. A few days later, to mark the first anniversary of the movement, JP urged the need to have a strong opposition to the ruling Congress party.

Jayaprakash Narayan addressing a large rally during the student protests of the 1970s

ANGER ON SCREEN

Amitabh Bachchan

The economic turmoil and discontentment of the 1970s also found its way into the cinema of the time. The villains in many movies such as Agneepath, Zanjeer, Trishul *and* Deewar *were rich businessmen or corrupt politicians, while the police were shown as helpless witnesses to social injustice. Heroes were people full of resentment, who blurred the lines between right and wrong in their quest for justice. Actor Amitabh Bachchan rose to fame during this decade, with his iconic portrayal of the 'angry young man'.*

An Embattled PM

Indira Gandhi was unnerved. In addition to the student protests and the growing might of JP, she was also troubled by an ongoing court case against her in the Allahabad High Court. Her opponent Raj Narain alleged that she had won the 1971 election in Rai Bareilly against him by using unfair means. On 12 June 1975, the high court found her guilty on two minor counts. Even though the charges made against her were trivial, calls for her resignation became forceful.

On 24 June, Indira Gandhi challenged the Allahabad High Court's judgement in the Supreme Court. But she wasn't allowed to take part in the proceedings of the Lok Sabha till the Supreme Court had resolved the matter. Embattled by the student protests and the court case, Indira Gandhi did the unthinkable . . . she demolished democracy and put India under a state of emergency.

12

It's an Emergency

The Constitution of India grants special powers to the central government to handle unexpected situations such as war and internal rebellion that endanger the country's security and the lives of its people. These are the Emergency provisions, under which the central government can take complete control of the country or a part of it and can curtail or suspend the freedom of citizens. The Proclamation of Emergency is issued by the Prime Minister and the council of ministers, and needs to be passed by the President.

Having made up her mind to declare an Emergency in India, Prime Minister Indira Gandhi acted fast. On 25 June 1975, an order declaring an Emergency was drafted. The President, Fakhruddin Ali Ahmad, who had been a supporter of Indira Gandhi, passed it as soon as it was placed before him.

The next morning, an unsuspecting nation, including ministers in her government, woke up to the news that India had been in a state of emergency since midnight. After informing her ministers, Indira Gandhi conveyed the news on All India Radio. In her address, she told people not to panic and said that the Emergency was a necessary response to a 'deep and widespread conspiracy' against her reform measures that sought to benefit ordinary Indians. She also clarified that she would lift the Emergency once conditions improved.

Indira Gandhi

Nevertheless, for the time being, Independent India was no longer a democracy. It was more like a dictatorship, firmly under the command of the Prime Minister and her government. Elections were cancelled and citizens lost most of the rights granted to them by the Constitution. In fact, the Constitution was deeply compromised because the government began amending it in order to secure its rule.

All the safeguards that had been put in place to prevent such a catastrophe were undone. Among the greatest of these was the judiciary that was forced to sit and watch the injustice unleashed by a government that took the law in its hands and used it to threaten anyone challenging its authority.

No Opposition

The Emergency was an extreme step, yet no one was allowed to question it. Anyone who could or would question the government landed up in jail without any trial. As soon as the Emergency was put in place, police swooped down on the government's political opponents, such as Jayaprakash Narayan, and imprisoned them. Throughout the course of the Emergency, thousands of such arrests were made. From political opponents to student activists—no opposition was spared. When the detainees demanded justice, the court turned them down, saying that the arrests had been made legal by the government of the day. A despairing editorial in a foreign newspaper remarked that the submission of an independent judiciary to an autocratic government was the virtually the last step in the destruction of democracy.

No Freedom of Press

One of the key Fundamental Rights suspended during the Emergency was the freedom of speech and expression. No one was allowed to speak against the government and this included the media. In those days there was no internet. Radio and television were limited and already under government control. It was primarily newspapers that were targeted.

On 25 June when the order declaring the Emergency was passed, power supply to all newspaper offices in Delhi was switched off. As a result of this, there were no newspaper editions on the 26th. Within a week of the Emergency, the government had set up a system of censorship under which it issued strict guidelines on what did and did not constitute 'news'. Newspapers were forbidden from running any story that was even mildly critical about the state of the nation or its administration. For example, there could be no reports on processions, strikes, political opposition or conditions in jails. Jokes ridiculing the government were especially banned. Dissenting journalists faced jail time. Newspaper owners feared that the government would shut down their presses or seize their properties. There was also the threat of power outages. But those toeing the line could benefit from generous payments received for advertisements placed by the government.

Strict censorship meant that newspapers often did not have enough news to fill the available space. Some decided to fill this gap with the words of the Prime Minister or stories praising her government. Others refused to oblige. They left white spaces in the place of stories that had been censored and reproduced reports on the Indian situation in the foreign press. When power was cut, they approached the courts. Sometimes, even the odd joke managed to slip in. For example, an 'obituary' among the classified ads in a newspaper announced the 'death of D.E.M. O'Cracy (Democracy), mourned by his wife T. Ruth (Truth), his son L.I. Bertie (Liberty) and his daughters Faith, Hope and Justice'. Stifled by censorship and the heavy cost of dissent, many small magazines closed down. This blockade on free press meant that news could not reach the people easily and they remained largely unaware of what the government was doing or what was actually unfolding in the nation.

State of the People

Even as opponents were imprisoned and the media was muffled, the streets remained strangely calm. There were no angry protestors to be seen. No strikes, boycotts or demonstrations. Shops and factories opened as usual and people set out for work. Public transport ran on time. The crime rate came down. A good monsoon in 1975 meant that food production increased and prices fell. There was a frenzied campaign to encourage discipline, punctuality, cleanliness and courtesy among the masses. It appeared as though a majority of Indians had no great interest in democracy and the freedoms it granted. Instead, they welcomed this new-found orderliness that made day-to-day life easier. Yet, discontent was simmering beneath the surface—and it was made worse by the coercive government programmes on family planning and slum clearance.

India's large and growing population had been a cause of great concern for many. They felt that a country with meagre means simply could not afford to meet the needs of so many people. Population control seemed to be the only solution. Under the cover of the Emergency, the Prime Minister's son Sanjay Gandhi began a programme of compulsory sterilization—a surgery that would stop people from having children. The campaign began in villages and towns in north India. It typically targeted poor families that had three or more children. Police vans took off the men from these families to the nearest health clinic for the sterilization surgery. Many men began to flee the vans. Those who could not escape and were forced to undergo the surgery were too embarrassed to speak of their plight. School teachers who were recruited to persuade people about the benefits of the campaign were greatly resentful. Many of them were jailed for resisting the order. Lower government officials had to produce a sterilization certificate to get paid. Truck drivers had to produce it to renew their licenses and slum dwellers would not be allotted plots for resettlement without it. While there were definitely benefits to family planning, the way the campaign was implemented incensed the masses. In some places, angry mobs set health clinics on fire, threw bottles and stones, clashed with the police and faced firing.

The other government programme that generated much opposition was the forceful demolition of slums that dotted Delhi. These had come up spontaneously and housed the families of sweepers, rickshaw-pullers, domestic servants, office boys and others who did low-paying jobs in residential colonies and government offices. The government wanted to knock down these settlements and move the inhabitants to farmland across the river Jamuna, which flowed through the capital. Clearing these dwellings was seen as a way of beautifying the city and raising its profile. However, instead of persuading the slum dwellers to shift, bulldozers were used to forcefully flatten their homes. When people resisted the bulldozers by squatting on streets, police were brought in to remove them. When the resistance grew, sticks, bullets and tear gas were used.

Slum demolition in Delhi during the Emergency

Resisting the Emergency

Even though the government came down heavily upon all those who disagreed with it, there were many who continued to resist. Within the Parliament, ministers made speeches of protest, walked out and boycotted sessions. On the streets, groups of people courted arrest by shouting slogans against the Emergency. There was also a growing underground resistance that sought to sabotage government plans and urged the people to rise against the regime.

Groups of writers secretly circulated literature satirizing the times. Others stopped writing in protest or shut down their publications before the government could do so. Many people returned awards such as the Padma Shri and Padma Bhushan, that the government had bestowed upon them.

Lifting the Emergency

On 18 January 1977—twenty-one months into the Emergency—the Prime Minister announced that the Parliament would be dissolved, and fresh elections would be held. The end of the Emergency came just as suddenly as its beginning. No one knows for sure what made Indira Gandhi lift it. Some say that having forcefully muted all opposition, she was convinced that she would be re-elected. Others say that elections in neighbouring Pakistan prompted her to indulge in competitive one-upmanship. Some feel that she was missing her contact with the people and longed for it. While others think that excessive criticism overseas made her reconsider her actions. Whatever may have been the reason, the Emergency was finally over. The government's opponents were released from prison. In the elections that followed, they formed the Janata Party, a joint front against the Congress led by Indira Gandhi.

For the first time after Independence, the Congress was voted out of power. The Janata Party that won the elections was an unstable coalition plagued by disagreements and could not last for an entire term of five years. Yet, it made a great contribution in restoring democracy. The Constitution that had been amended to enable the excesses of the Emergency was repaired and rectified, so that it became extremely difficult for any future government to think of imposing another Emergency upon the nation. Various commissions were set up to investigate the Emergency. The most influential of these was the Shah Commission under the former Chief Justice of India, J.C. Shah.

Social movements that had been interrupted by the Emergency re-emerged, and new movements, especially those advocating democratic rights, were formed. Censorship was dead and a 'newspaper revolution' was born, aided by new printing technology that came to India in the 1970s. This technology made printing easier, improved its quality and enabled multiple editions to be printed. Free of the draconian constraints that had been imposed by the Emergency, reporters and editors threw themselves into work with renewed vigour, and readers lapped up their hard-hitting stories about crime and political corruption. A readership survey conducted in 1979 found a rapid growth in readers, not just across geographies, but also across languages.

Democracy had prevailed. By voting out the ruling party that had imposed the Emergency, people had expressed their displeasure. The power of protest had gained momentum, as had the power of the press. One of the darkest episodes in Independent India's history had come to an end.

Mandal Commission

In 1979, the Janata Government set up a commission to identify the socially and educationally backward classes of India, also known as the Other Backward Castes (or classes), and make recommendations to address caste inequality and discrimination. It was headed by the politician B.P. Mandal and became popularly known as the Mandal Commission. By the time the commission submitted its report, the Janata Party was no longer in power. The report was buried and nothing came of it. But a decade later, in August 1990, Prime Minister V.P. Singh announced that his government was implementing one of the most basic recommendations of the commission. Henceforth, 27 per cent of all jobs in the central government would be reserved for candidates belonging to the other backward castes identified by the commission. Since 22.5 per cent of jobs were already reserved for candidates belonging to Scheduled Castes and Tribes, this new order meant that 49.5 per cent of all government jobs were now reserved for backward castes. The announcement sparked off violent protests by angry upper-caste students whose hopes for government employment had been undermined. Nearly 200 tried to commit suicide. Even though the protests eventually died down, the commission complicated the divide between people of different castes and became a landmark in caste-based politics.

Born into an illustrious family, Laila Tyabji was a young, freelance designer when the Emergency was declared. 'My parents' house was raided not because anyone thought they were hoarding black money, but as a general warning and intimidation that no one was safe from the authorities. The squad that came to search the house was so ignorant, blundering and incompetent that one felt the whole exercise was a farce.' The shocking curtailment of civil liberties in the days that followed prompted a streak of rebellion. She drove around Delhi in her little motorbike, distributing anti-Emergency leaflets. The brutal sterilization campaign, the forcible evictions and bulldozing of illegal colonies without notice had turned the government into an enemy who had to be evaded, bribed or tricked by any means possible. 'I think that divide is now built into the general Indian view of governments—of whichever party.'

13

Battling Disunity

In a country as diverse as India, differences and disagreements between people are common. But sometimes these become very serious and people from certain ethnic and religious minorities begin to feel alienated. This feeling often gives rise to violent separatist movements, or insurgencies, led by militant groups that demand autonomy and challenge the unity of India.

As a nation determined to preserve its unity at all costs, India has historically taken a forceful stance against separatist movements. When a state is gripped by such a movement and the state government is unable to control it, the state is put under President's Rule and comes under the control of the central government. It is declared a 'disturbed area' and the Armed Forces Special Powers Act (AFSPA) is imposed. Security forces flood the state and are given unprecedented powers to crush the insurgency. They can open fire on anyone perceived as a threat, arrest people on the suspicion of helping militants and search places without seeking any permission. No legal action can be taken against the security forces involved in such operations without the approval of the central government. This sometimes leads to excesses that threaten ordinary people of the state, who begin to feel trapped between the militants and security forces.

Insurgencies are born and bred amid the ordinary people of a state. So, addressing their fears and sense of alienation holds the key to unity and the possibility of lasting peace.

Over the years, there have been several reports of human rights violations under the AFSPA. For many people it has become a symbol of oppression. In 2000, Manipuri activist Irom Chanu Sharmila went on an indefinite hunger strike to protest against the act. She fasted for nearly sixteen years, during which she was force-fed through a nasal tube and imprisoned in a government hospital.

Origins of Discord

Although the insurgency in Kashmir that began in 1989 (*see page 217*) has often dominated headlines, the oldest insurgency in Independent India originated in the north-east. Comprising present-day Arunachal Pradesh, Assam, Manipur, Meghalaya, Mizoram, Nagaland and Tripura (collectively called the Seven Sisters), this region is home to hundreds of tribes with unique cultures. It is linked to India by a narrow strip of land, but shares large porous borders with Nepal, Bhutan, China, Myanmar and Bangladesh. Culturally and geographically distinct from the rest of India, it was kept largely isolated from the mainland under British rule. So, when the British left, many tribes of the north-east were reluctant to join the Union of India and sought their own autonomous homelands.

Armed rebellion for autonomy originated in Nagaland during the 1950s and swept through the region in the following decades. In many instances, militant groups found safe havens and support in bordering countries. Territorial claims and fights between different tribes added to the violence. During the 1960s and '70s, a large influx of refugees (*see page 12*) worsened the tension as native populations feared being overpowered by outsiders.

At the time of Independence, Meghalaya, Mizoram and Nagaland were part of Assam. Arunachal Pradesh was also governed by Assam, while Manipur and Tripura were princely states. The AFSPA was first imposed in 1958 to deal with the Naga insurgency. However, it was eventually extended to all north-eastern states. Although the central government was unwilling to grant autonomous homelands, it was willing to consider demands for statehood within the union of India. Beginning with Nagaland in 1963, different states were carved out in the north-east (*also see page 40*). Talks were initiated with various militant groups, and in several states, security operations were strategically planned to avoid excesses by the armed forces and build the trust of ordinary people. Meanwhile, various development projects, such as roads, railways and airports, were initiated to improve the geographical connectivity of the region to the rest of the country.

Over the years, these measures have helped control the insurgency in many states of the north-east. The AFSPA has been completely withdrawn in some states, and in 2022, the government announced that it was applicable only in certain districts of Assam, Nagaland, Manipur and Arunachal Pradesh.

Insurgency in the North-east

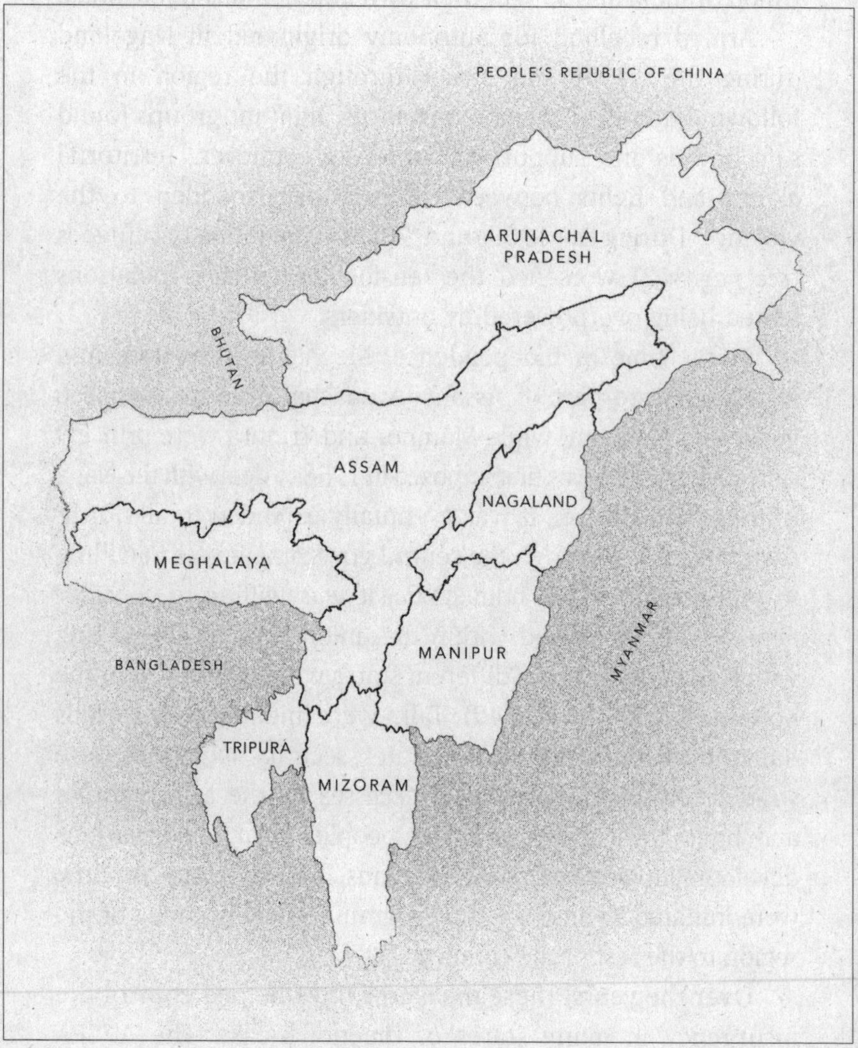

Source: Survey of India

Nagaland

- *Various Naga tribes continue demanding autonomy and laying territorial claims over areas in bordering states within the region.*
- *AFSPA: applicable in most districts*

Arunachal Pradesh:

- *Anger against Chakma and Hajong refugees (also see page 24)*
- *Militant groups, mainly from Nagaland, who used the state as a passage to the bordering countries of China and Myanmar, also aided the spread of separatism.*
- *AFSPA: applicable in some districts*

Mizoram:

- *Inability of the government to control mass starvation after a famine in 1959 led to a powerful uprising for autonomy.*
- *Became a separate state in 1987 and the insurgency effectively ended*
- *AFSPA: withdrawn*

Manipur:

- *A large number of militant groups representing several different tribes have been fighting against each other and also demanding autonomy.*
- *AFSPA: applicable in many districts*

Assam:

- *Violent agitation against Bengali refugees from Bangladesh (also see page 19)*
- *Bodo tribal groups demanding separate state since the 1980s*
- *AFSPA: applicable in some districts*

Tripura:

- *Violent agitation against Bengali refugees from Bangladesh*
- *Some militant groups demanding autonomy*
- *Successful counter-insurgency strategies controlled the violence*
- *AFSPA: withdrawn*

Meghalaya:

- *Migration from bordering countries, mainly Bangladesh, as well as other states, sparked anxieties*
- *Militant groups representing several different tribes have been fighting against each other and also demanding autonomy*
- *Successful counter-insurgency strategies controlled the violence*
- *AFSPA: withdrawn*

Problems in Punjab

The Sikh community had been hit hard by the Partition of Punjab in 1947. Large areas of their productive lands were now in Muslim-majority Pakistan, as was Nankana Saheb, the birthplace of Guru Nanak, the founder of their religion. Within India, they remained a small minority and felt sidelined by the Hindu majority. From the outset of Independence, they wanted a separate Sikh-majority state. After struggling for several years, this demand was finally granted in 1966 when the existing state was reorganized, with the hill-districts going to Himachal Pradesh, the Hindu-majority, Hindi-speaking areas forming Haryana and the Sikh-majority, Punjabi-speaking areas forming Punjab. However, the formation of a separate state did not solve all their problems. They had to continue sharing the Union Territory of Chandigarh with Haryana, as it remained the capital of both states.

In the elections held in 1977, the Akali Dal, a religious body and political party representing the Sikhs, won a majority of the seats in Punjab and came to power. A few years ago, the Akalis had made several demands of the central government. Among other things, they wanted Chandigarh and other Punjabi-speaking areas in neighbouring states to be handed over to Punjab. These demands were part of what they called the Anandpur Sahib Resolution. After winning the elections, they revived these demands and added new ones.

Even as the Akalis were raising various demands on behalf of the Sikhs, another more militant group was taking shape in Punjab to fight for the community. Leading this group was a Sikh preacher called Jarnail Singh Bhindranwale, who claimed that the Sikhs had become slaves to the Hindu majority in Independent India. He wanted the community to purify itself and return to the fundamentals of its faith. Bhindranwale disliked Sikhs who had veered away from traditional Sikhism and the five Ks: *Kesh* (uncut hair), *Kangha* (comb), *Kara* (bracelet), *Kachera* (cotton underpants) and *Kirpan* (dagger). He rapidly gained followers who identified with his religiosity and call for purification.

On 13 April 1978, there was a mass congregation of a religious sect called the Nirankaris, in Amritsar. Although the Nirankaris considered themselves Sikhs, unlike traditional Sikhs, they believed in a living Guru. While their congregation was being held, Bhindranwale preached an angry sermon that provoked many of his followers to attack the Nirankaris. Several people died in the clash. This incident is often marked as the beginning of a rising tide of separatist violence led by Bhindranwale's growing power over the Sikhs in Punjab.

Jarnail Singh Bhindranwale and his followers

Nirankaris, communists, government servants, political leaders, suspected informers, police and paramilitary personnel . . . armed groups of militants supported by Bhindranwale began to assassinate all those who disapproved of them or came in their way. Following the murder of an influential editor in 1981, an arrest warrant was issued against Bhindranwale. But three weeks later he was released for lack of evidence. His release only increased his hold over people who came to see him as a hero who had challenged and defeated the Government of India.

Till the beginning of the 1980s, no one paid serious attention to these violent 'fringe elements'. Instead, the Akalis continued negotiating with the central government on the Anandpur Sahib Resolution. Harcharan Singh Longowal, a new Akali leader, encouraged supporters to agitate for the Sikh demands listed under the resolution.

Operation Bluestar

As militancy grew, attacks on Hindus became more frequent. Meanwhile, the murder of high-ranking police officers demoralized the police force and crimes shot up. Several Hindus fled the state, while others formed their own defence force. Centuries of harmonious relations between Hindus and Sikhs were fraying under the militant violence. On 5 October 1983, militants stopped a bus on the highway, separated the Hindu passengers and shot them. Shortly afterwards, President's Rule was established and the AFSPA was imposed in Punjab.

In December 1983, Bhindranwale took up residence in the Akal Takht, situated within the Golden Temple Complex at Amritsar. The Akal Takht was a seat of Sikh religious authority. It was from here that the Sikh Gurus issued edicts that all Sikhs were required to honour, while Sikh warriors came here to receive blessings before going to war. The fact that Bhindranwale moved into this sacred building and no one had the courage to stop him was a dangerous indication of the times.

As Bhindranwale and his supporters began fortifying the Golden Temple Complex, the central government decided to act. At the beginning of June 1984, the army began moving into Amritsar. On 2 June, a young Sikh officer, posing as a pilgrim, entered the temple complex to observe and note the positions of the militants. That night, Prime Minister Indira Gandhi spoke on All India Radio, requesting the people of Punjab to maintain peace. On 3 June, Punjab was cordoned off from the rest of the country in order to prevent the militants from escaping. Road, rail and telephone links were cut off. In Amritsar, however, pilgrims were allowed to celebrate the anniversary of the martyrdom of the Sikh Guru Arjun Dev. The next day, loudspeakers were used to ask the pilgrims to vacate the complex. Firing began at night, as the army tried to knock down the militant positions. It hoped to seize the exteriors of the complex by midnight before moving into the Akal Takht and capturing the militants.

This was called 'Operation Bluestar'. It sought to rid the Golden Temple Complex of the militants within forty-eight hours, with no damage to the historic complex and minimum loss of life. Unfortunately, the operation grossly underestimated the number of militants, their skill, firepower and determination. The militants had clearly anticipated an attack by government troops and were more than ready for it. The troops were unable to break through their defences. So, they decided to use tanks.

On 6 June, tanks broke through the temple gates and rained fire on the Akal Takht. A fierce battle raged and by the evening Bhindranwale and his aides were dead. However, many innocent pilgrims were also killed in the crossfire and worst of all, the Akal Takht was heavily damaged. The Sikh community was shocked. Many wanted revenge for the mutilation of their holy shrine.

Operation Bluestar made the government realize that counter-insurgency needed a more discreet approach. Since then, special commandos have been trained for anti-terrorism operations.

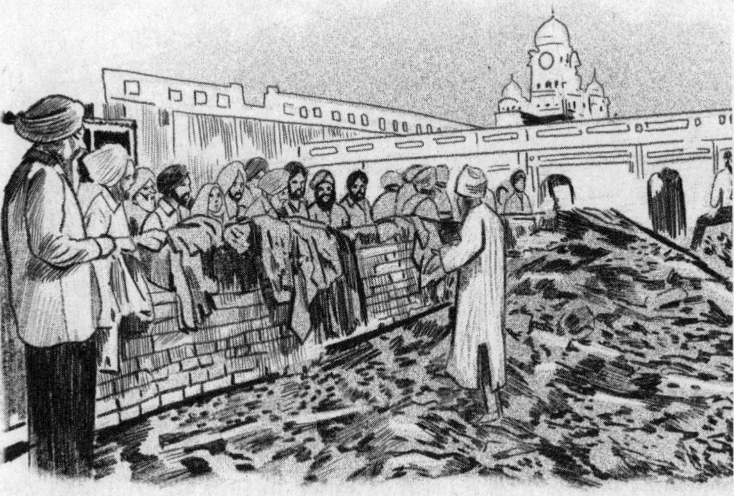

Sikh community shocked by the destruction of the Golden Temple Complex during Operation Bluestar

A few months after Operation Bluestar, on 31 October 1984, Indira Gandhi was assassinated by her Sikh bodyguards. All hell broke loose as her supporters, largely made up of various groups of Hindus living in and around Delhi, went on a rampage. They brutally murdered Sikhs, particularly Sikh males between eighteen and fifty years old, looted their shops, defiled their shrines and holy books. Attacks on Sikhs also happened in other cities and towns in northern India. Unfortunately, little effort was made to contain these on time. Finally, a curfew was imposed on 3 November 1984 and the army was called in to control the violence. Slowly, things crawled back to normal.

The anti-Sikh riots deepened the wedge in Hindu–Sikh relations and worsened the violence in Punjab. In July 1985, the new Prime Minister Rajiv Gandhi made an effort to resolve the situation by reaching out to the Akali leader Longowal.

An accord was signed. Among other things, it promised to transfer Chandigarh to Punjab, lift President's Rule and hold elections in the state. Following the agreement, Longowal toured Punjab asking people to support reconciliation. However, barely a month after the accord, militants assassinated him. They felt that he had betrayed the Sikhs by signing an accord with the central government. Nevertheless, elections were held in Punjab. Longowal's assassination had created a wave of sympathy for the Akalis and an Akali government led by Surjit Singh Barnala came to power. But it was unable to control militancy and violence continued unabated.

Operation Black Thunder

In April 1986, militants recaptured the Golden Temple and began fortifying it. They made an open declaration of an armed struggle for Khalistan—a separate Sikh nation. The government refused to negotiate with them. By May 1987, Punjab was under President's rule once again. A year later, in another operation called 'Black Thunder', the army cleared about fifty militants from the complex. Unlike Bluestar, this operation was relatively bloodless and did not damage any structure within the complex. The militants, in this instance, were neither as well-prepared nor as motivated as Bhindranwale's men. Trapped inside the temple by the assault, they had desecrated its interior with filth and their capture did not lead to any massive protest.

Slow Return to Normalcy

In 1992, President's rule was again lifted and an election was held in the presence of thousands of security personnel.

Voter turnout was extremely low and a Congress government headed by Beant Singh came to power. Meanwhile, under the leadership of K.P.S. Gill, the Punjab police used other measures to curb militancy. Huge bounties were placed on the heads of militant leaders to motivate their capture, while a more lenient approach was taken against the ordinary fighters. So, when their leaders were captured, many ordinary fighters surrendered.

Apart from the unrelenting suppression of their movement, the militants were also gradually weakened by internal differences, distrust and infighting. Most importantly, over time, they lost legitimacy with the ordinary people of Punjab, who came to view them as criminals engaged in robbery, extortion, rape, indiscriminate killings and terrorist attacks against civilians. Stuck between the militants and state oppression, the people began their own resistance against militancy by refusing to be cowed down by it. By the mid-1990s, militancy had crumbled rapidly in Punjab, and in 1997, the AFSPA was withdrawn.

Merits of Diversity

In 1948, the British military commander Sir Claude Auchinleck remarked that India was not a nation but a continent of many nations. Sooner or later, it was bound to break up. Even though several separatist movements have emerged in India since Independence, and groups of people, such as Nagas and Kashmiris feel alienated, the country remains home to many different people. Despite various predictions of its break-up, the landmass remains united and no part, as yet, has fallen away.

India's pluralism resides in reassuring citizens that being 'Indian' doesn't mean giving up on their other identities. So, one can belong to any religious or ethnic group but still be Indian. The unity of India lies in nurturing this pluralism and building the trust of those who feel alienated.

As a doctor at the main government hospital in Chandigarh, S.K. Gupta found himself smack in the middle of the violence playing out in Punjab during the insurgency. Post-mortems of the dead and treating the grievously injured, including militants, were a regular affair. As a Hindu, it was hard to ignore the religious tension, but as a doctor he could not allow differences and fears to get in the way. To his utter surprise, many of the militants turned out to be such polite young boys that it was hard to imagine them killing or injuring anyone. He feels that unemployment might have pushed them into militancy. Besides, as he found, Bhindranwale was an exceptionally captivating man. 'I saw him at the Golden Temple during the initial years of the militancy. He was this tall man with an imposing presence and alluring smile. It was easy to imagine why someone might hero-worship him.' Till today, the doctor has many Sikh friends who admire Bhindranwale despite the violence he unleashed against Hindus in the state. Yet, they remain friends. 'We have decided to respectfully agree to disagree and not rake up matters that can injure the many other joys of our friendship.'

14

The World's Worst Industrial Disaster

Independent India had faced Partition, wars, droughts, mass starvation, angry protests, insurgencies . . . but in 1984 it faced a disaster unlike any other. A large area in the city of Bhopal was enveloped in a cloud of poisonous gas that leaked out of a factory and thousands of men, women and children died a most gruesome death as the nation watched helplessly.

Union Carbide India Limited

In 1969, an American company called Union Carbide set up a factory in Bhopal to manufacture pesticides for India's Green Revolution (*also see page 115*). These pesticides were made using dangerous chemicals, including methyl isocyanate (MIC). There was nothing unusual in this. Chemical pesticides are made of dangerous chemicals. The problem was that the factory wasn't safe. Workers had complained of faulty equipment and poor operation and maintenance. There had even been a few accidents within the factory. Yet no one took safety issues seriously. The factory neither had a suitable early-warning system nor any emergency plans. Everyone appeared ignorant of the hazards posed by the dangerous chemicals it used. What was even worse was that the factory was located in the midst of a sprawling settlement, occupied mostly by the city's poor. So, in ignoring safety, the factory owners had not only risked the lives of the workers, but also of the large population living around the factory.

Disaster Strikes

On the night between 2 and 3 December 1984, water leaked into a giant tank of MIC and set off a chemical reaction that released a large quantity of poisonous gas. Dangerously high pressure began to build up inside the tank. The workers were so used to faulty equipment that many of them thought something was wrong with the pressure-recording instruments! By the time they realized the enormity of the leak, it was too late.

Union Carbide factory in Bhopal

At 1 a.m., when the first public siren began to blow, it had been nearly an hour since deadly gas had escaped from the factory. A foul smell filled the air. People living in colonies around the factory woke up coughing violently. Their eyes and skin were burning as if someone had thrown chilli powder on them. Breathing became increasingly difficult. The first patient at the nearest hospital arrived around 1.15 a.m. An hour later, there were 4000. The staff was shocked and confused. They didn't know what to do with the patients, and Union Carbide was not giving away any information about the gas that might have helped in the treatment. Soon, many hospital staff were also overwhelmed by the gas and became too sick to work.

At 3 a.m., a second siren began to blow. By this time, there was a stampede on the streets as hundreds of people tried desperately to leave the city. They got on to whatever they could—cycles, bullock carts, tempos, trucks . . . Overwhelmed by the poison, they vomited, bled and many simply suffocated and died. When the sun rose, death was everywhere—in homes, hospitals and streets—and room to cremate or bury the dead was running out rapidly.

The gas that had escaped the factory took several days to dissipate. If not for the two lakes in the area where it eventually dissolved, it would have spread over a longer distance, and claimed many more lives. However, the horror wasn't over. Several tonnes of the deadly gas were still trapped inside the factory. At 8.30 a.m. on 16 December, a much-publicized operation was conducted to neutralize it. So much gas was trapped that instead of the expected four to five days, the operation took a week. The people mistrusted the authorities. Fearing for their safety, over 1,00,000 left the city before the operation.

Ongoing Suffering

By the last week of December, Bhopal was gas-free, but it wasn't free of the effects of the gas. Thousands of people had died of suffocation and life was hell for those who survived. From breathlessness to eye pain, there was no end to their health issues. Many of them were so sick that they could not get up from bed. Having lost all their strength, they could neither do housework nor earn their livelihood.

Thousands of cattle and other animals had been killed by the gas. But there was no one to clear the carcasses as many municipal workers had fallen sick. The army and workers from outside had to be deployed for this work. Many carcasses had swollen up so much that houses had to be broken down to remove them.

On the sixth day after the leakage, several people were rushed to hospitals in a serious condition. Doctors believed they had fallen sick because of eating fish from the lakes in the area. The main fish market was immediately sealed and slaughterhouses were closed down so that the meat of gas-affected animals could not be sold. A few weeks later, a swarm of green flies invaded the gas-affected areas, attracted by the improperly disposed carcasses. There were fears that an epidemic may break out because of the unsanitary conditions prevailing in the colonies around the factory.

Failing the People

Union Carbide did not disclose details of the composition of the gas that had leaked out of its factory. This made effective treatment of the victims difficult. Moreover, vast quantities of toxic waste that had been dumped in and around the factory remained in the environment, polluting the soil and groundwater.

The company's neglect of safety was compounded by the government's failure in managing the disaster efficiently. On the second day after the gas-leak, it was broadcasting that everything was safe, and things were returning to normal! The free distribution of milk and ration was badly organized, as were rehabilitation measures such as skill development and housing. In the end, these measures left a large number of victims untouched.

In 1985, the Indian Council of Medical Research (ICMR) began a study on the health impact of the gas on those exposed to it. But this was eventually discontinued, and its findings were not released to the public. Even the medical records of the victims were not properly documented. So, even though deadly diseases like lung cancer are commonly reported in the area and adverse health conditions have passed down through generations of the original gas victims, there is insufficient research to link this to the leakage. Till today, there is no name for the disease caused by the gas, no clear identification of its victims or the status of their treatment. The health infrastructure that was increased over the years to tackle the growing health crisis also proved to be largely futile in the absence of sufficient medical knowledge of the poison and qualified doctors. Moreover, people found neighbourhood clinics and dispensaries far more accessible than the new facilities.

The single biggest ground for anger against the government has been the distribution of compensation to the victims of the tragedy. In its initial panic, the government rushed payments and awarded lakhs of rupees to over 5000 victims. However, on 7 December, it suspended this disbursement and following a house-to-house survey, payments began to be made through cheques. But many victims were so poor that they didn't have bank accounts to deposit and encash the cheques. Moreover, the paperwork for claiming compensation was cumbersome and tiring. Although such measures were adopted to discourage unscrupulous claims, they ended up doing more harm than good.

In the aftermath of the tragedy, the factory was closed down, a few company officials were arrested and an inquiry was initiated into the accident. The Government of India filed a case against Union Carbide for claims amounting to USD 3 billion, but in a big blow to the victims, in 1989 it settled all claims against the company for USD 470 million. The victims tried to overturn the settlement but were not successful. Meanwhile, the company did everything in its power to dilute its responsibility in what happened. Till today, many gas victims continue protesting against the injustice done to them by the company as well as the government.

Victims of the Bhopal Gas Tragedy and their families continue protesting against the injustice done to them

Quest for Justice

The Bhopal gas tragedy opened India's eyes to the perils of industrialization, especially factories working with hazardous raw materials. This led to the landmark Environmental Protection Act (EPA) of 1986, under which the government can restrict the setting up and operation of any industry that has the potential to harm the environment and endanger lives.

Even though India has not seen another Bhopal-like disaster, industrial accidents continue to haunt it. In the last decade alone, the country has witnessed over 100 accidents involving chemicals that have claimed over 250 lives and injured more than 500 people. Protests against industries have been reported in the media time and again. Unless institutions involved in environmental governance, like Pollution Control Boards, are strengthened and laws such as the EPA are enforced more strictly and effectively, justice will continue to elude people who are worst affected by industries that degrade their surroundings and threaten their well-being.

In June 2010, India became the third country in the world after Australia and New Zealand to set up a National Green Tribunal (NGT)—a court made up of people with a legal background and those with expertise on environmental issues. It is dedicated exclusively to environmental cases relating to matters like pollution, forest conservation and providing relief to victims of industrial accidents involving hazardous materials. To find out more about the NGT, visit http://greentribunal.gov.in

PART 4

TOWARDS A NEW INDIA

15

Where's the Money?

During the sixteenth century, India was the richest country in the world. The Mughal Emperor Aurangzeb reported an annual revenue of 100 million pounds in the year 1700! So, it wasn't surprising that traders from around the world were lured to India. Among them were the British traders of the East India Company. Bit by bit, they spread their influence across the land and came to rule over it. Close to two centuries later, when the British finally left India, it was a desperately poor country.

Industrialized Britain had drained India's wealth to meet the needs of its own industries. Instead of food, farmers were compelled to grow large quantities of crops like cotton, jute and indigo, which became cheap raw materials for its factories. To make things worse, they were forced to pay huge taxes for cultivating land. Agriculture was ruined by this merciless exploitation of farmers. Food shortages were rampant and devastating famines broke out. Apart from farmers, India's skilled craftsmen, who made some of the most exquisite handmade products, such as cloth, jewellery and handicrafts, were left penniless because the market was flooded with cheap, mass-manufactured products from

Britain's factories. By the end of British rule, India was an impoverished, underdeveloped country that hardly made anything on its own.

Uplifting India

The leaders of Independent India had their job cut out for them. They had to make India self-reliant so it didn't have to depend heavily on foreign countries. Modern industries had to be built so India could produce all the things it needed and offer greater employment opportunities to its people. Agriculture had to be revived to uplift farmers and address the dire food shortages. This was an enormous undertaking.

India began to build dams for irrigation and clear more land for farmers to cultivate. The government initiated land reforms to make farmers the owners of land and stopped taxing them (*also see page 112*). It set up various industries producing basic and heavy industrial goods, such as coal, iron, steel, shipbuilding and aircraft production, to reduce India's dependence on imports. The production of consumer goods, such as clothing, furniture and personal care products, was left to small privately run cottage industry firms that depended on manual labour and offered employment to a large number of people. Most of all, it started building basic infrastructure, such as roads, power plants and educational institutions, that was absolutely necessary for development. In a country as backward as India, every new development was celebrated as a sign of progress. Jawaharlal Nehru called factories, research laboratories, dams and power stations the 'temples of modern India'.

Development is an expensive exercise and the kind of development newly independent India had undertaken, needed a lot of money. So, it had to plan its expenses carefully. In 1950, the government set up a Planning Commission to prepare five-year plans for social and economic development. These plans outlined how the government was going to spend its money on nation building.

Hard Times

In order to finance its development, newly independent India had to take big loans. Money was always tight. One of the biggest problems was India's inability to afford enough foreign currency, mainly the US dollar, that it needed to import, or buy, the things it wanted from foreign countries, such as industrial machines and materials. A US dollar is worth several rupees. So, every time India spent dollars on imports, its coffers were depleted. The country wasn't able to earn sufficient foreign currency because it didn't have much to export, or sell, to foreign countries, at the time.

The first crisis came in 1958. Its coffers were running so low that India was facing a situation where it would neither be able to pay for imports nor return the money it had borrowed for its development. Even though India managed to evade this crisis by tightening expenditure, cutting back on imports and seeking monetary aid, the problem was far from over. India's expenses kept mounting unexpectedly through the 1960s and '70s. It fought wars and had to spend heavily on defence. Back-to-back droughts led to acute food shortages and vast quantities of food grains had to be imported to prevent mass-starvation. There was a large influx of refugees from East Pakistan (now Bangladesh) who had to be provided for. Then, there were the oil shocks that began in the 1970s. Problems in the Middle East—the largest oil supplier in the world—hit supplies and raised oil prices. Since India was importing most of its oil, it ended up spending a bulk of its money on this.

Even though the Green Revolution in the 1960s (*also see page 115*) helped India produce sufficient food grains to feed its people, this was not enough to solve its problems. The economic turmoil had led to rising poverty and unemployment, which increased people's anger and disillusionment with the government.

In a bid to prevent the situation from spiralling out of its control, the government began to take over more and more industries, such as banking and coal mining. The system of issuing licenses to the private sector to start new companies was made so stringent and cumbersome that it came to be called 'Licence Raj'. Refusing to give in to the increasing government control, a few prominent multinational companies, such as IBM, closed their operations in India. Meanwhile, under government protection and in the absence of competition, small firms manufacturing consumer goods became complacent. Quality suffered, quantity was barely enough to meet the demand, and prices shot up. But Indian consumers had no option. They were forced to make do with what was available. For some goods, like scooters, the supply fell so short that buyers had to wait for several years after placing an order. This was a time when Indians developed a craze for anything 'imported'—since it was automatically associated with 'high quality'!

These changes neither improved India's economic growth nor did they address the challenges of poverty and unemployment. By the 1980s, it became clear that the government did not have the capacity to run the economy. Even though it had managed to take charge of the economy in the initial years after Independence, this became unsustainable as the population increased and the government's work expanded. Guidelines on granting and denying permissions to the private sector under the License Raj were often unclear. As the volume of applications increased, inefficiency crept in alongside corruption. Bribery became rampant as did unethical business practices. Big business houses with deep pockets and close connections to the government were at an advantage and managed to corner most licenses, while smaller companies suffered. Meanwhile, government-run companies often ran into losses and even other sources of government income, such as taxation, failed to generate sufficient revenue. India needed to allow more private companies to come in and increase imports to meets its growing needs.

Big Changes

Today, India is one of the fastest growing economies in the world. It has billions of dollars' worth of foreign currency. Private companies outnumber government enterprises. Most of the world's biggest multinational companies have an office in India and many Indians are employed by them. Its markets are dominated by foreign brands like Coca Cola, Samsung and Apple. The beginning of this transformation goes back to the 1980s, when the government started to gradually reduce its iron-grip over the economy. However, the biggest change came about in 1991 when the country was beset by the worst economic crisis since Independence. It barely had enough foreign currency to buy three weeks' worth of imports and its borrowings had spiralled out of control . . .

The new government that had come to power in 1991 was shocked by the depth of the crisis. There was no time to waste. Prime Minister Narasimha Rao called upon economist Manmohan Singh to sort out the mess. The reforms that followed were extreme for an economy that had protected itself from the world for nearly three decades.

Narasimha Rao (L) and Manmohan Singh (R)

Singh saw that the only way out was for India to open its doors and allow the world to step in. Foreign goods and services began to flow into its markets. The government stopped protecting most local industries. They had to be able to fight the competition on their own merit and become good enough to beat it. License Raj was demolished. The government needed to run the country more than running companies. So, it began welcoming private companies for business and even sold off many of its own companies to private firms. Several foreign firms began to invest in India and set up businesses here. To replenish its depleted coffers, the government pledged large amounts of the country's gold in exchange for foreign currency.

With each passing decade, these changes continued to proliferate, increasing India's economic might and global significance. Indeed, when he announced these changes in 1991, Singh said:

> *'No power on earth can stop an idea whose time has come . . . the emergence of India as a major economic power in the world happens to be one such idea. Let the whole world hear it loud and clear, India is wide awake. We shall prevail.'*

Five-year plans were discontinued in 2015. In a rapidly changing economy, it became difficult to formulate such long-terms plans that would bind the government and suit everyone across the country. The National Institution for Transforming India (NITI Aayog) replaced the Planning Commission.

India witnessed several changes in the years following the economic reforms of 1991

A few years after Independence. . .

Today . . .

'It felt like good news after a very long time,' says K.R. Prithviraj, reminiscing on the economic reforms of 1991. 'Like someone had finally done something about India's problems.' But the changes crept in slowly. New brands were advertised in the media. New products could be seen in shops. New shops opened up. New eateries came up. New companies came in, offering new jobs to people . . . By the end of the decade, Prithviraj found himself and many others around him earning more money than ever before, with many more things to spend it on. As a man born in 1947, he was used to living in a country where money was tight and austerity had been a way of life. 'We weren't stingy. We were simply not used to having much money.' When the reforms were introduced, he was in his forties and found it difficult to spend money on all the new things that looked like luxuries to him but became necessities for the children in his family. 'They are living in an India that is nothing like the one in which I spent more than half my life. They would be miserable if they were living in the India of my youth. You had to wait several months, if not years, just to get a telephone connection!'

Fighting Inequality

Few deny that the reforms of 1991 helped to lift a large number of Indians out of destitution. They led to the growth of a significant middle class that lies between the extremes of penury and privilege in modern India. Yet, crores of Indians continue to struggle with scarcity.

Most of India's growth since 1991 has come from the services sector that has witnessed a big boom, especially on account of information technology (*also see page 199*). Since a majority of service sector enterprises are clustered around cities, their growth has prompted dramatic and largely unregulated urbanization in India. Big cities such as Bengaluru, Delhi and Mumbai are crumbling under the pressures of overpopulation, as large numbers of people migrate to them in search of better job opportunities. Urban infrastructure such as housing, water supply and waste disposal remains woefully inadequate. It is predicted that by 2050, about 60 per cent of India will live in cities instead of rural areas. Unless urban infrastructure is improved, the quality of life for a majority of Indians living in these areas will remain dismal despite the economic growth.

Even as the service sector has boomed, the sharp decline in agriculture and slow growth in manufacturing have been worrisome, because these sectors employ far more people. Seven decades after Independence, agriculture continues to suffer from inadequate irrigation. Even though India no longer witnesses acute food shortages as seen in the past, declining development in agriculture has thrown up an intense spate of farmer suicides since the 1990s. Most of these are on account of crop failure and indebtedness. Meanwhile, the manufacturing sector has suffered on account of increased competition from foreign imports. In a bid to improve efficiency and competitiveness, many factories have replaced human labour with machines, which has reduced employment opportunities for workers. Some of the poorest people in modern India are those who labour in its farms and factories. They earn less, work in poor conditions and are constantly under the threat of losing their jobs (*also see page 237*).

The true measure of a country's wealth is its people and the things they can grow, make or produce with their hard work. After all, it's through the buying and selling of these very things that a country generates wealth. Having money would mean little if nothing was being bought and sold. That's why economic development must lead to social development. If a country's coffers are stuffed, but its people are poor, undernourished, uneducated and unhealthy—sooner or later its progress will decline.

Independent India's spectacular economic success will remain incomplete if it's not able to help its people build better lives. Increased incomes would amount to nothing if people are unable to meet basic needs like nutritious food, good education, quality healthcare and housing. Nobel prize-winning economist Amartya Sen says that India is perhaps the only country trying to become a global economic power with an uneducated and unhealthy workforce. Having successfully filled its coffers after struggling for several decades after Independence, it now needs to use this money to reduce the inequality in its society. Unless it is able to do this, he fears that one half of India will come to look and live like California while the other will resemble sub-Saharan Africa.

16

Technology Comes Home

Free India was born in a world assailed by the might of technology. The Second World War, which ended a few years before India's independence, had been a terrifying display of the power of machines over humans. Soon afterwards, the world was thrust into a cold war between hostile groups of countries led by the US and the USSR. From weapons to spacecraft, in the years after the war, these groups competed against each other to corner the best technologies for themselves. But where was Independent India in this race for technology?

Newly independent India was a largely rural land living in a time warp. Most of its people didn't even have access to electricity, let alone modern technology. For a large mass of Indians, technology implied simple everyday objects, such as bullock carts, ploughs and spinning wheels. Used to manual labour, they mistrusted the modern world and its quest to replace humans with machines. In the words of Mahatma Gandhi, '*Machinery merely helps a few to ride on the back of millions. The impetus behind it all is . . . greed.*'

Despite this resistance, India began its pursuit of technological advancement with ambitious programmes in nuclear energy (*see page 84*) and space (*see page 95*). Small groups of eminent scientists and planners worked in laboratories and prestigious research institutions, such as the Indian Institute of Science and the Tata Institute of Fundamental Research. But what of the people? How were ordinary Indians introduced to the wonders of science and technology?

The Need for Scientific Temper

Back in the 1940s, just about 12 per cent of India's people could read and write. Jawaharlal Nehru feared that without necessary education, Indians might not understand the purpose of technology and would be overwhelmed by it. So, he encouraged the establishment of a wide network of institutes across the country to educate people in science and technology. Among these were the Indian Institutes of Technology (IITs), modelled after the prestigious Massachusetts Institute of Technology (MIT) in the US. The first IIT was inaugurated at Kharagpur, West Bengal, in 1951.

In addition to establishing education institutions, Nehru wanted scientists and engineers working on major nation-building projects to engage with ordinary workers and explain to them the purpose of what they were doing. On observing hundreds of workers carrying baskets of mud for the construction of a dam, he asked the engineers if the workers had been explained the reason for the work they were doing and its significance. Similarly, he placed great emphasis on training programmes for Indian engineers so they would not become beholden to the machines they were using—most of which were imported.

During the 1950s, India also initiated community development programmes that sought to familiarize farming communities with improved methods of livestock rearing, irrigation and agriculture, aided by the supply of electricity, water, roads and transport. Nehru called these 'higher techniques' and urged the communities to master them as a first step to understanding modern technology. Although these programmes fizzled out as they failed to generate enough local participation, desperate food and milk shortages in the '60s and '70s led farmers to engage with new technologies, changing the face of agriculture and dairies in India (*also see pages 116* and *125*).

While the government made various efforts to introduce 'scientific temper' to the masses in the initial decades after Independence, it did not encourage the active adoption of technology by ordinary Indians for several years. It tended to view electronic devices for everyday use as 'luxuries' and placed various restrictions on them. Heavy taxes were imposed on these devices, making them prohibitively expensive. But in doing so, it had misread the pulse of the people. The history of technology in India is in many ways the story of various consumer electronics that found a firm footing in the daily lives of Indians and redefined the ways in which India viewed itself and the wider world.

An Ear to the World

Among the oldest forms of mass-media, radios were first introduced in India during the 1920s. A preserve of the elite, the first radio broadcasts were made by fancy radio clubs in Bombay, Calcutta and Madras. But these broadcasts cost too much money and didn't last. In 1930, the British government set up the Indian Broadcasting Service, which became All India Radio (AIR) in 1936. At the time of Independence, AIR had stations in Delhi, Bombay, Calcutta, Madras, Tiruchirapalli and Lucknow, in addition to three others in Pakistan. Nehru's iconic 'Tryst with Destiny' speech, updates on wars, cricket commentaries, Indira Gandhi's announcement of the Emergency . . . radio conveyed the state of the nation to listeners and found a growing audience.

An early radio set

For most listeners, the allure of radio lay in film songs. But the government felt that these songs were far too 'westernized' and would be a negative cultural influence. In 1952, it banned film songs on AIR and decided to replace them with Indian classical music. However, listeners would have none of this. They turned to Radio Ceylon that was broadcasting all the way from Sri Lanka to tune into its legendary musical show *Binaca Geetmala*, which was dedicated entirely to

Indian film songs. The show would air every Wednesday from 8–9 p.m. and avid listeners would drop everything else to enjoy the music, sing along and jot down lyrics. Its massive popularity compelled AIR to lift the ban on film songs in 1957 and begin a new radio channel that offered a non-stop broadcast of Indian film music!

Tune in

Wondering what these 'westernized' songs were that the Indian government banned back in the 1950s? You could search for film music from this period on the internet and hear it yourself to decide! One possible source could be https://www.hindigeetmala.net/geetmala/.

By the 1960s, the government was well aware of the rising popularity of radios. In a speech at Roorkee University, Prime Minister Indira Gandhi spoke of how transistor radios in the hands of bullock-cart drivers was 'not an uncommon sight'. She also acknowledged that apart from information and music, the radio was 'a symbol of modernity and the world of plenty'. Advertising too was introduced on AIR in 1967. Still, the government remained disinterested in promoting consumer electronics like radios. Despite this, the number of listeners continued to increase as did sales of radio sets and offerings by AIR.

By the 1980s, the government began to gradually loosen its restrictions. In the 1990s, it invited private players to begin their own radio stations and in 2001, *Radio City* Bangalore became India's first private FM radio station. Today, there are several such radio stations available across India, such as *Radio Mirchi* and *BIG FM 92.7*. You can listen to radio using sets installed in cars or even on the internet. Gone are the days when people had to spend a lot of money to buy bulky radio sets to tune into their favourite radio channels.

In 2002, the government granted permission for setting up community radio stations. Ordinary Indians could operate these radio stations, producing and broadcasting programmes relevant to local communities. One the first community radio stations was established at Anna University in Chennai, in 2004. It catered to the needs of people residing around the university with broadcasts on issues such as healthcare, female literacy, employment and clean environment. Since then, there has been a proliferation of community radio stations in educational institutions as well as small towns and districts across India.

The phenomenal spread of radio in India is intertwined with the history of another piece of broadcast technology that grabbed eyeballs and hooked Indians in the years after Independence . . .

An Eye to the World

Television came to India almost accidentally. Following an exhibition in Delhi, the multinational company Philips sold the TV equipment that it had imported for the event to the Indian government at an extremely low cost. This equipment was supplemented with additional offerings from the US as well as a grant from the United Nations Educational, Scientific and Cultural Organization (UNESCO) to purchase more. Using all this help, India began an experimental TV broadcast in September 1959.

Fewer than 100 TV sets existed in India at the time, and coverage was limited to Delhi. Two hour-long programmes were aired every week. These were usually educational programmes for school children and farmers that focused on themes like health and citizens' duties and rights. With hardly any presence compared to the radio, TV began life as another broadcast medium under AIR. The only channel available on it was Doordarshan (DD), a Hindi word for 'distant vision'. But in the 1970s, the government began to pay greater attention to it. TV stations were opened in other parts of the country and in 1976, DD became independent of AIR. Gradually, television began to supplement radio as a major source of entertainment, but it was only in the 1980s that it came into its own, aided amply by advancements in broadcast technology.

The year 1982 marked a major milestone in the history of Indian television. That year, India hosted the Asian Games and in the run-up to the event, it eased restrictions on the import of colour televisions for screening the games. Thousands of sets poured into the market and Indians discovered the joys of live, colour broadcasts for the very first time. Soon, television coverage began to expand rapidly as people tuned in to watch everything from sports, soap operas and movies to blow-by-blow coverage of various events. Two programmes that found millions of viewers and broke all telecast records were the dramatized versions of the Hindu epics—the Ramayana and the Mahabharata—that were aired on weekends. Streets and marketplaces were reported to be empty when the shows were on air.

By the end of the 1980s, DD dominated viewers and earned large revenues through advertising. But in the 1990s, it was forever challenged by the coming of cable networks that expanded the watchlist on TV, exponentially. BBC, CNN, MTV, Zee, Star . . . various private and international channels were beamed in Indian homes. Many young Indians fell in love with the American sitcom *Friends*, which first aired on Indian television in 1999 and brought home the exploits of six young New Yorkers struggling with issues around relationships and careers. From foreign accents to glamorous clothing and different ways of life—television proved to be addictive, exposing viewers to diverse cultural influences that gave them bigger, bolder dreams.

A group of people watching Ramayana on TV during the 1980s

Computing Comes of Age

Radio had existed in India before Independence and television caught on by the 1970s, but computers largely remained outside public consciousness till the 1980s. In tech-wary India, they were viewed with much suspicion. When the Bombay office of the Life Insurance Corporation (LIC) installed a computer on its premises in 1963, protests broke out against these 'job-eating' machines. Such protests continued to gain momentum through the 1960s, forcing the government to publicly denounce technology. However, it was impossible to ignore computers in the pursuit of development.

As early as 1960, scientists in India had developed the country's first computer, TIFRAC (Tata Institute of Fundamental Research Automatic Calculator) and were working on other homegrown models. The loss to China in the 1962 war had made India painfully aware of its technological inadequacies, especially in the sphere of electronics. Almost every major defence system in the modern world was powered by electronics that India thoroughly lacked. In order to address this deficiency, the government initiated indigenous production of electronics and also set up a high-level electronics committee. Among other things, this committee claimed that computers were 'leading to the development of a new outlook and . . . scientific culture.' So, even as protests brewed outside, various government and private enterprises as well as educational institutions were gradually acquiring computers for their work.

Since computing technology in India was nascent, it was an American company IBM (International Business Machines Corporation) that dominated the country's computing market in the initial decades. But in the 1970s, its operations came under a government scanner. Worsening economic conditions in the country had prompted the government to tighten its leash over various industries. For the first time, the government set conditions for IBM if it was interested in continuing its Indian operations. This led to IBM exiting India on 1 June 1978. But its exit posed a big problem. What was going to happen to the large number of IBM machines in India? Who was going to service them now? In overcoming this challenge, India saw the rise of some of the biggest companies in Indian computing, such as Wipro, TCS (Tata Consultancy Services) and HCL (Hindustan Computers Limited).

In 1984, forty-year-old Rajiv Gandhi became India's sixth Prime Minister. A technology buff, he was keen to erase the old suspicion against machines, particularly computers. The only way to do this was to integrate them into the daily lives of Indians. One of the first things Rajiv Gandhi did after assuming his post was announcing a new computer policy that eased restrictions on computer imports. Thousands of relatively cheap personal computers flooded the Indian market. Despite the opposition, the government launched technology projects that brought computers closer to the people. One of these was the computerization of the passenger reservation system of the Indian Railways. The reason you can find everything from train schedules to tickets online today is because of this project that was launched in 1986.

As the wall between citizens and computers began to melt, India unlocked its knack for software—the various applications, scripts and programs that allow computers to function. Armed with affordable computers, more and more Indians discovered their skills in programming, while Indian computing enterprises realized just how lucrative these skills were. Unlike India, developed countries in the West had come to depend so heavily on computers that they were in urgent need of programmers—a need that India catered to, with its economically-priced, growing talent pool in software. In the run-up to the year 2000, the beginning of a new millennium, technologically advanced countries in the West found themselves facing a peculiar problem. Their machines were threatened by the 'millennium bug'—and they turned to Indian programmers to fix it!

How would you write the date 1 January in the year 2000 in numerals? You would think that it should be written as 01/01/2000 in the day-month-year format. But what if you were prohibited from writing down the full year, and could only put in the last two digits of the year? This would mean that this date would read as 01/01/00 in numerals. What's '00' supposed to mean, you might wonder—the end of time? This was the trouble that technology landed in, during the run-up to the year 2000. Computers around the world had been programmed to read dates in the problematic 01/01/00 format. If this wasn't corrected, computers could end up reading 01/01/2000 as 01/01/1900 and any computer activity that was programmed on a daily or yearly basis would be flawed. For example, if a customer applied for a loan on 1 January 2000, the computer might calculate the rate of interest based on 1 January 1900! Similar problems could affect flight records and computerised safety checks at power plants . . . An army of Indian programmers went through a massive number of computer programs, correcting the date problem in each.

Possibly for the first time in its history, Independent India became a saviour for the developed world. Instead of 'job-eating' machines, computers came to be widely perceived as 'job-creating' machines in the country. Lured by the unprecedented employment opportunities, India took to computers like no technology before. In selling its software skills to the world, India built a giant 'outsourcing' industry that has been fuelling its economic growth since the 1990s.

Children milling around a computer

The rise of computers was followed closely by the launch of the internet in India on 15 August 1995. The opening up of cyberspace to ordinary Indians proved to be a turning point in the history of technology in India. Initially limited to computers, the internet grew and grew, offering all manner of services—online education, banking, shopping, paying bills, booking tickets—on all types of devices. One such device that unleashed a full-fledged technology revolution was the mobile phone.

'We were nerdy kids,' reminisces Karan Mahajan, while talking of his childhood in Delhi. Growing up in the 1990s, Karan and his younger brother, Shiv, found a useful outlet for their youthful energy in a newly acquired, internet-enabled personal computer. Fans of players like Sanath Jayasuriya, the Waugh brothers and Sachin Tendulkar, and enamoured by the glamour surrounding cricket, the school boys launched a website featuring statistics and colourful commentaries on matches. 'We were obsessed with the game. We would play cricket at home and school, watch it on cable TV, discuss it with friends, chat about it with random strangers on the internet and write about it on our website.' Their mini enterprise, Indian-cricket-fever.com, became so popular that in 2000, the teenagers were recruited by the world's largest sports network of the time, rivals.net, as its official cricket reporters for India! The 'job' came with many more readers, boasting rights at home and school, and a princely pay of 200 pounds a month. Although the website is now a defunct relic of their childhood, it led them both to their future calling. While Karan discovered his passion for writing and became a successful novelist, Shiv stuck to tech and built a thriving career in programming.

'Smart' Phones

In July 1995, Jyoti Basu, the Chief Minister of West Bengal made the first mobile call in India. From his office in Calcutta, he called and spoke to Sukh Ram, the communications minister based in Delhi. The device Basu used was a boxy little Nokia phone and the network was primitive. Yet, the call marked the beginning of a service that connected India in a way landlines never could.

Like most new technologies, in its initial years the mobile phone was an expensive proposition—beyond the reach of most Indians. The handset was priced at over 20,000 rupees and call charges were over 8 rupees per minute! But as more and more Indians discovered the convenience of carrying phones with them and remaining in constant touch instead of relying on fixed landlines, mobile phones started getting popular. New phone models became available in the market, costs began to fall, features began to improve and networks began to increase. By 2004, the number of mobile phone connections had overtaken landlines. A decade later, internet-enabled, advanced mobile phones or 'smartphones' had put more computing power into the hands of average Indians than the most powerful computers that existed in India's laboratories during the '60s and '70s.

For many Indians, the smartphone was not just their first computer, but also their first music player, TV and camera—technologies they hadn't been able to afford earlier. It brought a world of internet-enabled knowledge and services into their hands. The Internet that was originally 'made-in-English' had found one of its largest audiences among multilingual mobile phone users in India. So, its content was made available in various Indian languages such as Hindi, Tamil and Bengali. Things went one step further with a voice activation feature that allowed people who could neither read nor type to command their phone by simply speaking to it. Today, about 60 crore Indians own a smartphone and India has the highest rates of internet consumption on mobile phones.

For Vimla, a fifty-five-year-old domestic helper who only studied till Class 5 and hardly had any access to technology growing up in rural India, the smartphone was nothing short of magic. When her son bought the phone in 2017, she wasn't particularly enthused by it. In fact, she laughed in disbelief when he asked her to speak to it. 'I thought he had lost his mind,' she reminisces. Still, with everyone's nudging, she asked it to play her a Hindi song—and it started playing it! 'I never thought that something like this would be possible,' she says. Today, the phone is her most prized possession. 'My daughter and I can talk to each other any time without others listening to our conversation. We usually speak to each other outside our homes. It's too small and crowded inside and you can't talk in peace. I can call my employers when I'm running late or need a holiday. When I feel low or troubled, I find a quiet place and ask my phone to play me a song or video. Recently, I've been learning some new recipes on it. The only problem is my five-year-old granddaughter, who snatches it from me the moment I get home. She's so young and still she manages to operate it. I think in the next generation, babies will begin using such machines the moment they roll out of their mothers' wombs.'

Harnessing Technology

In the years since Independence, India's technology story has become the stuff of legends. Technology that had aroused various doubts and suspicion has become a source of national wealth and prestige. Yet, once it's unleashed, technology tends to grow faster than it's understood or analysed. So, it's hard to determine what purpose it might eventually serve.

Many technologies that have enhanced our lives were originally used in warfare. For instance, ultrasound technology that can detect illness inside the human body was used in war to detect underwater submarines. Similarly, social media platforms such as WhatsApp and Facebook, which were meant to create communities online, have not only helped people to connect with friends but have also been used to spread rumours that fan unrest and spark violence.

As more and more Indians get captivated by the power of technology, and Indian homes equipped with all manner of electronic gadgets become showpieces of the country's technological advancement, it's important to remember that technology is driven by human agency. Its worth lies not in its abilities but in the choices we make while using it.

17

One Nation, Many Religions

Partition of British India into Hindu-and-Muslim-majority countries had filled many people of both the communities with hatred against each other. Despite this provocation and rage, India refused to pin its identity to being a Hindu-majority nation. Instead, it chose to remain a secular country that embraced people of all religions, including Muslims. For the leaders of Independent India, Partition was a warning against communalism—using religion to divide people—and how it could destroy unity and break up nations. However, in a country where religion is said to be all important, the path of secularism has been riddled with numerous challenges. While there have been various communal episodes in the history of Independent India, such as the separatist strife in Punjab (*see page 161*), the most persistent differences have cropped up between Hindus and Muslims, haunted by the wounds of Partition.

One Law for All Religions?

For a long time, India had a set of personal laws relating to matters such as marriage and inheritance that were particular to different sects and religions. The leaders of Independent India wondered if replacing these separate laws with a Uniform Civil Code that applied equally to people of all religions would help secularism. But the time wasn't right. The country had just been through Partition. Communal feelings ran high and minorities, especially Muslims, felt vulnerable. Yet, in an effort to lay the ground for it, a uniform code was proposed for India's largest community—the Hindus. This was called the Hindu Code Bill and it applied not only to all Hindus, but also to Sikhs, Buddhists and Jains.

The bill was opposed heatedly both within and outside the constituent assembly. Its opponents felt that Jawaharlal Nehru, B.R. Ambedkar and other leaders supporting the bill were discriminating against Hindus by interfering with their personal laws and pandering to the Muslims, by neither touching their personal laws nor imposing a Uniform Civil Code on them. In the run-up to the first elections held in 1952, an anti-Hindu-Code-Bill movement picked up pace. The agitators called the bill 'an atom bomb on Hindu society'. During the elections, a man named Prabhu Dutt Brahmachari stood opposite Nehru in Allahabad. He was supported by various Hindu communal parties and his entire campaign was based on one promise—if he won, unlike Nehru, he would not tamper with Hindu tradition. But this didn't work and he lost heavily. Communalism had been unable to sway voters. After the elections, Nehru was formally appointed India's Prime Minister and eventually the legislature under him passed the bill.

Even though communal issues failed to dominate electoral politics in the early decades, things began to change in the 1960s, especially after the death of Nehru. The Congress, which had been the single largest political party, began to face tough competition from other political parties. As voters began to get more and more divided, political parties pulled out all stops in a bid to woo them. A few prominent issues that emerged in the 1980s and thereafter, captured public imagination in a big way and became landmarks in the history of communalism in Independent India. Incidentally, among the first of these brought back the debate on personal laws and the Uniform Civil Code.

The Tale of Two Muslim Women

In April 1978, a sixty-two-year-old Muslim woman named Shah Bano filed a petition at a local court in Indore, demanding a monthly maintenance from her husband Mohammed Ahmed Khan following their divorce. The two were married in 1932 and had five children. However, Khan, a renowned local lawyer, married again and asked Shah Bano to leave his house. Unable to support herself and her children, she approached the court. Her husband contested her claim by stating that under the Muslim Personal Law, he was only required to support her for three months. The case dragged on. It went to the High Court, which ordered Khan to pay her a monthly maintenance of Rs 179.20. In 1981, Khan took the matter to the Supreme Court. After deliberating on it for four years, the Supreme Court rejected his appeal in 1985.

Instead of applying the Muslim Personal Law, the Supreme Court invoked the general law under which a man with sufficient means was required to provide a monthly maintenance to his divorced wife if she was unable to support herself. In passing this judgement, the court took note of different religious laws but, irrespective of them, chose to uphold gender equality.

The decision of the court enraged Muslim religious leaders who felt that by overruling the Muslim Personal Law, the court had attacked their religion. Shah Bano was denounced by members of her community and demonstrations were held outside her house. In November 1985, she placed her thumb impression on a statement claiming that she opposed the interference in the Muslim Personal Law and would donate the maintenance money to charity. The incident was whipped up during various by-elections held at the end of 1985, in which the ruling Congress was trounced. Under pressure, the government passed the Muslim Women's (Protection of Rights on Divorce) Act in May 1986, which overturned the Supreme Court's decision and gave credence to the Muslim Personal Law. The burden of supporting a divorced wife unable to support herself was placed on her family members and the husband was only required to pay maintenance for three months.

Close to three decades later, another Muslim woman, Shayara Bano, approached the Supreme Court. Her husband had divorced her by stating the word 'talaq' three times in a row. Although this practice of 'triple talaq' was recognized by the Muslim community, Shayara found it unjust and wanted the court to abolish it. Her petition was supported by various women's rights organizations like Bebaak Collective and Bhartiya Muslim Mahila Andolan. Eventually, in 2017, the court declared the practice unconstitutional. Despite this, it continued. So, in 2019, the ruling Bharatiya Janata Party (BJP) passed the Muslim Women (Protection of Rights on Marriage) Act. Under this law, 'triple talaq' was declared a punishable offence, under which the husband could be fined and imprisoned for up to three years. However, many people did not support the introduction of a criminal punishment like imprisonment in a personal matter like divorce.

The petitions of Shah Bano and Shayara Bano not only posed questions on the Muslim Personal Law, they also raked up the need for a Uniform Civil Code to bring uniformity on personal matters related to marriage, inheritance, etc. However, even after seventy-five years of independence, the idea of having a law that governs all personal matters of citizens irrespective of religion remains contentious. Many sections of the population continue to feel vulnerable and believe that the implementation of a Uniform Civil Code goes against the spirit of secularism.

Demolition of the Babri Masjid

The town of Ayodhya in Uttar Pradesh had a large mosque called the Babri Masjid, built in the sixteenth century by a general of the Mughal Emperor Babar. But there was also a small Hindu shrine located within its premises. Hindu groups called it *Ram Janmabhoomi*—the birthplace of the Hindu god Ram—and claimed that the mosque had been built after demolishing a temple. Muslim groups denied this claim. This made the site a fertile ground for religious tension between Hindus and Muslims. The first recorded instance of communal tension over the site dates back to the 1850s. During the British era, the conflict was handled by effecting a compromise, whereby Muslims continued worshipping inside the mosque, while Hindus made offerings on a separate raised platform.

In 1949, fresh tensions broke out after an idol of child Ram (*Ram Lalla*) emerged at the site. Activists representing the two communities approached the court, asking it to decide on the matter. Eventually, the site was closed. But in 1984, a Hindu organization called the Vishwa Hindu Parishad (VHP) began a fresh campaign to allow public worship of the idol at the Babri Masjid. Hundreds of monks from numerous temples in Ayodhya were brought under its banner. Processions and public meetings were held and fiery speeches were made. A local lawyer approached the district court, and in February 1986, the court ordered the locks to be broken to permit worship. Many believe that the ruling Congress at the centre had allowed this verdict to appease the protesting Hindu groups. Unfortunately, the opening of the locks didn't end the protests. Instead, this only emboldened the protestors who now wanted the mosque to be demolished and a temple to be built in its place.

As the campaign gained momentum, it also became a political issue championed by the BJP that had emerged in the 1980s. In the Lok Sabha elections held in 1989, the party won eighty-six seats—more than ever before. The very next year, it began a *rath yatra*, a procession that started at the ancient temple of Somnath in Gujarat and was to conclude, five weeks later, at Ayodhya. It was led by the BJP leader L.K. Advani, who was travelling in a Toyota van that was made to resemble a chariot. The procession ended in frightening violence. Advani and various other participants were imprisoned, brutal clashes broke out with security forces that had been put in place to prevent the procession from reaching the mosque. The incident incited communal passions and the state of Uttar Pradesh was rocked by religious riots. In the elections that followed in 1991, the BJP won even more seats.

In July 1992, an investigation team found that demolition had begun at the mosque and a large platform was being constructed. The new government at the centre, a coalition led by the Congress, tried to settle the matter by holding meetings with VHP leaders. But nothing came of these. Instead, the VHP announced that on 6 December it would begin constructing the temple. Anticipating trouble, thousands of paramilitary troops were assembled near Ayodhya. But these were never called in and it was left to the state police to control the large group of Hindu *kar sevaks* (volunteers) who began gathering in the town. The plan was to hold a prayer on the raised platform that had been built. But the *kar sevaks* ended up storming and demolishing the mosque. In a single afternoon, a centuries-old structure was brought down violently in the name of religion. A big contention was that this was a monument protected by the government. Then how was it allowed to be torn down by the mob?

Kar sevaks climb on top of the Babri Masjid and begin its demolition

The demolition of the Babri Masjid became a turning point in the history of communalism in Independent India. Religious riots broke out in more than sixty cities and thousands of people were killed and injured. Among the worst hit was the city of Bombay, where a curfew was imposed and the army had to be called in. It took more than a week for the situation to be brought under control. But the peace was temporary. In March 1993, a terrorist and criminal mastermind Dawood Ibrahim retaliated against the demolition by coordinating a series of bomb blasts that ripped through the city.

Communal tension seized the country. Many wondered if Hindus and Muslims could ever learn to live together again. In 2002, savage riots broke out in Godhra, a town in Gujarat that had a troubled history of communal violence. Meanwhile, a series of court battles played out over the temple versus mosque issue in Ayodhya, even as the Archaeological Survey of India (ASI) began excavating the site to inspect whether the mosque had indeed been built over a temple.

In 2010, the matter was finally taken to the Supreme Court. After deliberating on it for close to a decade, the court passed its verdict on 9 November 2019. Even though it condemned the barbaric demolition of the mosque, it said that the ASI's excavation had revealed that the mosque had been built over a structure whose architecture was indigenous and non-Islamic. As such, it awarded the disputed land measuring close to three acres for the construction of a temple. However, it also ordered five acres of land to be allocated in Ayodhya for the possible construction of a mosque. Although the issue had been settled by the court and the construction of the temple began in 2020, the deeply communal history of the dispute has continued to raise questions on the fate of minorities in a Hindu-majority nation.

Insurgency in Kashmir

Jammu & Kashmir was a Muslim-majority princely state in British India, and its story after Indian independence began with a strident call for autonomy (*see page 33*). This led to Article 370 of the Constitution, which allowed the state to independently control all matters apart from defence, foreign affairs and communications—giving it greater autonomy than other states within the Union of India. It was allowed to have a separate state flag, its Chief Minister was called Prime Minister and people from outside Kashmir were prohibited from buying land or property within it. These were major concessions and many residents of the state, especially in Hindu-majority Jammu, became uncomfortable with them. During the 1950s, the Praja Parishad, a local party in Jammu, began agitating against the special privileges granted to the state under Article 370, with the catchy slogan '*Ek Desh Mein Do Vidhan, Do Pradhan, Do Nishan—nahin chalenge, nahin chalenge*' (Having two constitutions, two heads and two flags in one nation will not work). They wanted it to be completely integrated with the Union of India. Their demands were also supported by Dr Syama Prasad Mookerjee, a national leader who had founded the Bharatiya Jana Sangh, which eventually became the BJP.

Although little came of this agitation except renaming the position of Prime Minister to Chief Minister, Article 370 began to get diluted bit by bit. The people found that the central government continued to meddle in their affairs. This became most evident in the poor record of democracy in Kashmir. Free and fair elections were largely missing. The elections of 1987 were among the worst, with several instances of vote rigging. Large numbers of Kashmiris were deeply disillusioned. In a quest for autonomy, many of them began moving away from the government and towards militancy. Unfortunately, the militancy painted the quest for autonomy in communal colours.

Kashmiri Pandits, who had co-existed peacefully with the Muslims of the Valley thus far, became targets of the militants. Many of them were killed brutally in the militant uprising of 1989–1990, prompting a mass exodus of Pandit families from Kashmir to Hindu-majority Jammu as well as other parts of India. This worsened communal tension in the country.

The rapidly growing militancy prompted the Centre to impose the Armed Forces Special Powers Act (*also see page 155*) and flood the state with security forces. In an effort to crush the militants, these forces used extreme forms of aggression that worsened the wedge between the government and Kashmiris.

Although several separatist groups were active in the state, by the 1990s, the liberation struggle for Kashmir—labelled *jihad*—fell largely under the control of the Hizb-ul-Mujahideen, Islamic extremists who supported the merger of Kashmir with Pakistan. Not surprisingly, the rising militancy was actively aided by Pakistan. It ran training camps for militants, supplied weapons and more infiltrators. Life in the Valley changed dramatically under the influence of the extremists. Cinema halls and video parlours were closed. Drinking and smoking were banned. Women were forced to veil themselves and acid was thrown on those who resisted. Suicide attacks against security forces became increasingly common. By 1995, the state was effectively sandwiched in a war between the militants and security forces.

Following the insurgency, violence became common in Kashmir

In 1998, India and Pakistan tested nuclear weapons and declared themselves nuclear-weapon states. This added an alarming angle to the conflict in Kashmir that had already spurred two wars between the countries, in 1947 and 1965. Yet, hostilities ran so high that both countries went to war again in 1999. Even though India emerged victorious, the impending nuclear threat led to a lot of international pressure over the issue. Leaders of both countries were compelled to try and settle their differences. But the militancy thwarted all efforts at peace. In February 2019, forty Central Reserve Police Force personnel were killed when militants rammed an explosive-filled vehicle into a bus ferrying them. The attack led to a wave of anger across India. Close on its heels came the most hotly debated action by India in the history of insurgency in Kashmir.

At the beginning of August 2019, thousands of additional Indian troops were stationed in the Valley, a major Hindu pilgrimage was cancelled, schools and colleges were shut, tourists were ordered to leave and local political leaders were placed under house arrest. Telephone and internet services were suspended to cut off all communication lines. On 6 August, Article 370 was revoked. The government claimed that the state was finally integrated with India and there was no question on granting autonomy to it. But it remains to be seen if this fundamental change in the status of Kashmir is able to resolve the troubled legacy of this dispute.

When Safina Nabi thinks of her childhood, she recalls the intense anxiety of growing up amidst gun-toting men in uniform, making announcements on loudspeakers. She remembers street fights, curfews, bloodshed and the perpetual fear of violence. As a girl born in Kashmir, at the onset of the insurgency, her childhood was anything but normal. Solace usually came in the form of television serials and Bollywood movies. 'I used to reprimand my grandfather for always wanting to watch the news. It felt like a waste of time. People were dying every moment. You didn't need the news on TV to remind you of this.' In hindsight, it strikes her that she had started talking almost casually of death as a child. But in Kashmir, she says, children grow up before they come of age.

Fate of Secularism

Questions over personal laws, demolition of the Babri Masjid and the insurgency in Kashmir have all increased differences between Hindus and Muslims. For many, the victory of the BJP in the Lok Sabha elections of 2014 and 2019 is further proof of the rising might of Hindutva—the idea of India as a Hindu-majority nation instead of a secular land. Emboldened by its victory, some groups have been increasingly targeting minorities through a variety of campaigns, such as reconverting Hindus who had turned to Christianity and Islam and attacking Muslims for alleged cow slaughter, in the name of protecting cows that are revered by the Hindu religion. The resilience of India's secularism has been bitterly tested by such events.

In a world beset by various differences between people, unifying ideas such as secularism have been challenged throughout history. However, the fate of such ideas is shaped by people. So long as Indians do not allow themselves to be defined primarily by their religion, communalism will not prevail. If we continue to appreciate the things that unite us and celebrate our diversity—TV serials, Bollywood movies, literature, music, food—secularism will persist, and we shall continue to be enriched by the incredible plurality of our land.

18

Electrified!

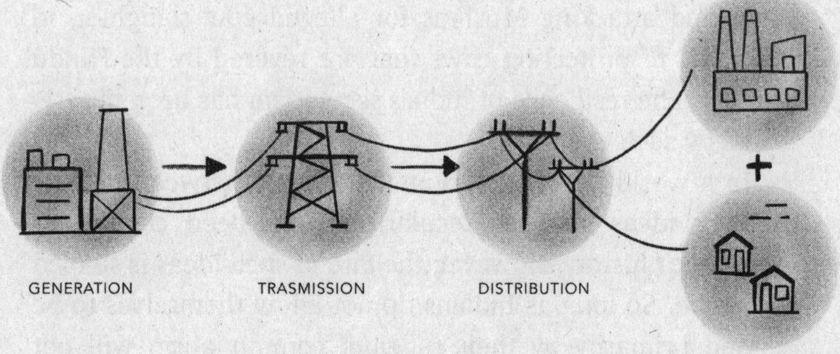

Electric grid

In May 2018, a tiny village in Manipur lit up with light bulbs for the very first time. After seventy-two years of independence, Leisang had been added to the National Electric Grid. A few months later, on Independence Day, the government declared that India had finally been electrified . . .

Electricity generation only began in the 1800s and was introduced in India by the British. It was produced by private companies and largely restricted to urban and industrial centres in modern day Maharashtra, Tamil Nadu, West Bengal and Karnataka. At the time of Independence, most Indians lived in rural areas that had never witnessed electricity. They used *pankhas* (hand fans) to keep themselves cool and oil lamps for lighting.

Electricity for Social Good

The leaders of newly independent India believed that electricity was the most necessary and revolutionary thing one could take into rural areas, for it could change the life of people. It could make factories hum. It could help irrigate farms. It could light up public spaces and dispel the problems of darkness. With this belief in the social good of electricity, the government took over electrification and began to spend large amounts of money on generating and taking electricity to all parts of the country. Each state set up a system of generating, transmitting and distributing electric power. This was a massive technological exercise that spanned several decades. It was not until the late 1990s that India had a National Electric Grid that connected producers and consumers of electricity across different states.

In 1963, Shanta Bijawat's village near Jaipur finally got electricity. Sixteen-year-old Shanta, who loved sewing, could now stitch fabric day and night without worrying about the poor light of oil lamps and the constant danger of fire. Lighting remains the most transformative change in her life. 'I find it easier to clean, cook and wash by hand. I don't like using electronic gadgets to do my work. They make people inactive. But I cannot live in darkness any more. A light is always switched on in my house.'

Electricity in India

>99 per cent

households connected to the grid

>20 hours

power supply to the average household from the grid. Urban areas get more than rural areas.

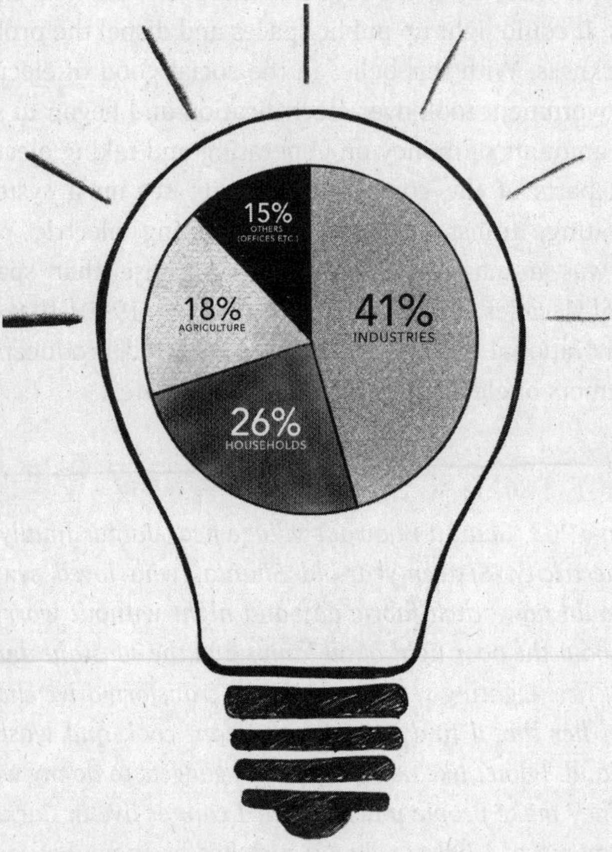

Electricity usage in India

Source: Council on Energy, Environment and Water and the National Power Portal

Sourcing Electricity

Coal-fired thermal power plants and hydroelectricity from massive dams were at the centre of Independent India's pursuit of electrification. After all, the country had significant reserves of coal and many large rivers. In addition to these, it was also investing large sums of money on nuclear power (*also see page 86*). The entire focus was on generating and supplying as much electricity as possible. No one really thought much about where this electricity was coming from. But a rude shock in 1973 compelled the world to think in this direction.

Fossil fuels like coal and oil power most of the world, generating electricity and fuelling transport. A majority of the world's oil comes from the Middle East. Even India spends a lot of money on buying it. In 1973, a war in the Middle East disrupted oil supplies for much of the world. The price of oil increased dramatically and the expense put a major dent on India's coffers. One effect of this 'oil shock' was that it forced countries around the world, including India, to look more seriously at other sources of energy to power their growth. Moreover, fossil fuels are non-renewable. Once they run out, they cannot be replaced. The Earth has such vast quantities of these fuels that the world has been using them non-stop for hundreds of years. The oil shock forced countries to think—what if fossil fuels ran out? How would they manage?

By the 1980s, much of the world was actively pursuing renewable energy drawn from sources that nature has an endless supply of, such as sunlight and wind. One of the major reasons driving the push for renewable energy during this decade was a growing worry around global warming. Several countries were reporting unusually high temperatures, heatwaves and droughts. Fires broke out in the Amazon rainforest. The world was heating up and burning fossil fuels to produce energy was a major reason behind this. Not only did it emit smoke, it also released carbon dioxide, a gas that trapped the sun's heat in the Earth's atmosphere and raised temperatures. Unless steps were taken to control carbon-dioxide emissions, the world would become unbearably hot, endangering the future of all living beings.

'Clean' Energy

India set up an independent Department of Non-conventional Energy Sources in 1982, which eventually became the Ministry of New and Renewable Energy in 2006. From biomass (plant and animal matter) to wind and sunlight, it began exploring electricity generation from various renewable sources. Today, it has some of world's largest wind and solar power plants and has seen an extraordinary increase in its capacity to generate electricity from renewable sources. However, humanity has depended so long on fossil fuels that switching to an entirely new source of energy will take time. Yet, our need for electricity is surging by the day and the dangers of climate change loom large. Finding alternative ways of powering development has become most urgent.

Since 1992, countries around the world have been gathering at major international summits to discuss ways of combating climate change by controlling their carbon emissions. Initially, it was felt that developed countries that had been at the helm of the industrial revolution should take responsibility and cut their emissions. India agreed with this. After all, developing countries that began industrializing much later had to be given a fair opportunity to grow. Forcing them to reduce their emissions would halt their industrial growth and economic progress. Besides, these countries contribute a much smaller percentage of global carbon emissions. But at the Paris Climate Conference in 2014, India agreed to cut its own emissions instead of insisting that developed countries cut theirs first.

Among the goals it has set for itself is to meet about half of its energy requirements from non-fossil fuels by 2030. This is an ambitious target that requires a remarkable transformation in the ways in which we generate, transmit, distribute and consume electricity. The process has already started. Over the past few years, India has developed a significant capacity to generate electricity from renewable sources and it remains to be seen how India uses this to overcome its dependence on fossil fuels.

Wind turbines

Solar panels

Renewable Energy in India

2070
the year by which India hopes to achieve net zero emissions

7 per cent
India's share of global carbon emissions

<8 per cent
electricity currently generated from renewable sources

>39 per cent
capacity to generate energy from renewable sources, mostly solar and wind

>70 per cent
electricity currently generated from non-renewable fossil fuels.

Source: News reports on COP26, data from World Resources Institute and the Ministry of Power

Conserving Electricity

In addition to developing renewable sources of energy, India has also been working on energy efficiency since the 1980s—ways of using lesser energy to achieve the same level of development. In 2001, the government passed a landmark Energy Conservation Act that has popularized energy efficiency among consumers. Buildings, factories, households . . . the push for using electricity judiciously is all around us.

If you observe appliances such as refrigerators or air-conditioners, you might find a star rating on them. The more the number of stars, the more energy-efficient the appliance. So, if the appliance has a four-star rating, it uses less energy and automatically reduces your electricity bill. Similarly, mobile phones and laptops come with a power-saving mode. Many residential buildings, hotels and offices are also actively promoting energy-efficient ways of lighting and cooling. For example, many of them are being built in ways that avoid using too much lighting during the day and power is promptly turned off after office hours to prevent wastage.

Power Cuts

In July 2012, the national electric grid suffered a major collapse. About 60 crore people in twenty-one states across the country went without electricity for two successive days. Trains came to a halt. Cars, trucks and buses clogged roads as traffic signals stopped working. Houses, shops, factories and hospitals lost essential power supply. The event grabbed headlines in national and international media. One of the world's fastest growing economies had failed to deliver what was seen as a basic need. Indeed, the promise of *bijli* (electricity) had been figuring high among election promises made by various political parties since the 1970s. So why had India failed?

In the initial decades after Independence, India focused heavily on industrialization and a large amount of subsidized electricity was provided to industries. With dire food shortages and the coming of the Green Revolution in the 1960s, the government began to provide subsidized electricity for agriculture. This was used to operate pump sets that drew out groundwater for irrigation. By the 1980s, with the growth of electrification, demand for electricity began to surge across the country. Expenditure on electrification increased, but subsidies crippled revenues for government bodies engaged in the generation, transmission and distribution of electricity. As they ran into losses, supply began to fall short of demand. In a bid overcome this challenge, the government started encouraging the production of electricity by private producers during the 1990s. This eventually led to the landmark Electricity Act of 2003 that allowed buyers and sellers to produce and consume electricity independently.

Although these changes increased the production of electricity, transmission and distribution continue to remain a challenge. A large amount of electricity is lost before it can reach consumers because of faults in the grid and power thefts by stealthy connections. Power outages have haunted India for several years and a constant, uninterrupted supply of electricity is still a long way off. Many buildings and factories have installed generators that work like mini power stations to ensure a backup in case of electricity failure from the grid. Meanwhile, local or regional sources of power have helped in taking electricity to places that are still not connected to the grid. As India gets about 250 to 300 days of sunshine in a year, solar power has been especially popular. Since 2010, rooftop solar panels that can independently power homes and buildings are becoming increasingly visible in cities as well as villages across the country. But maintaining these systems and ensuring that they work smoothly has been an uphill task.

In a quiet corner of Chennai is a house that runs eleven fans, twenty-five lights, a refrigerator, computer, water pump, TV, mixer-grinder, oven, washing machine and an AC entirely on solar energy! For the past few years, it hasn't had a single power cut. The owner who built this highly effective system is fondly called 'Solar' Suresh!

Electricity for All

The pursuit of electrification in the years since Independence has been deeply transformative. Lighting has helped reduce household fires caused by oil lamps. Children are able to study after dark and education levels have improved. People can continue working till late and increase their income. Crime rates have fallen and it has become safer to venture outside after dark.

Despite this, many households continue to remain without electricity. They are neither connected to the grid nor do they have access to any local sources of electricity. This is not always because of insufficient generation or inadequate transmission. Very often the distribution of electricity is also impacted by social divides. Richer neighbourhoods in cities and wealthier households in villages almost inevitably have greater access to electricity because they are able to pay for it and it is presumed that they need it more because they have the money to afford technology that runs on electricity. This is truly unfortunate because electricity usage is a cornerstone of modern development. Until every last household in the country has access to affordable electricity, irrespective of its geographical location or social standing, India's quest to become a global superpower will remain incomplete.

Pandemic Years and Beyond

On 30 December 2019, Li Wenliang, a doctor in Wuhan, China, allegedly posted a message on the Chinese messaging app WeChat, informing his medical school alumni group about an infectious new virus that was on the prowl. The very next day, the Wuhan health authorities announced a viral outbreak and alerted the World Health Organization (WHO). However, they reprimanded the doctor for 'spreading rumours online' and 'disrupting social order'. A week later, the doctor had succumbed to the virus.

On 13 January 2020, a Chinese woman was quarantined in Thailand. For the first time, the virus had been reported outside China. Soon, reports of infected patients were pouring in from countries around the world. Towards the end of January, a patient in a hospital room in Thrissur, Kerala, learnt from a television news report that the first case of the virus had been detected in her hometown. She had no idea that the report was in fact referring to her! A medical

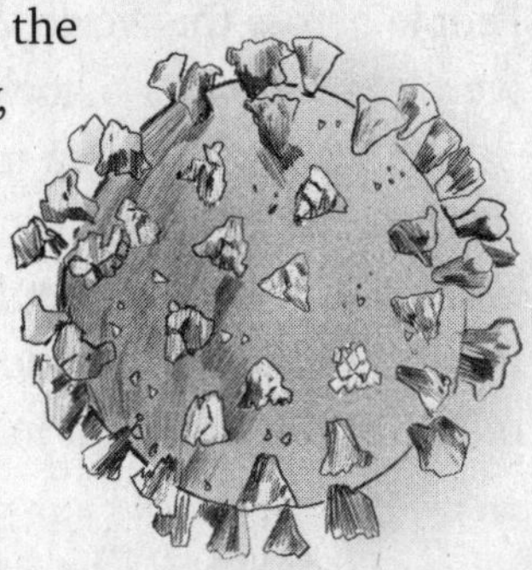

COVID-19 virus

student at the Wuhan University, she had returned home six days earlier after learning of the mysterious virus that was infecting people across China. On 3 February, the Kerala government declared a state calamity, after two more cases were reported. The next day, India cancelled visas for Chinese visitors and foreigners who had visited China in the previous two weeks.

On 10 February, the WHO named the virus COVID-19. By then more than 40,000 people had been infected and over 1000 had died across various countries. A month later, on 11 March, COVID-19 was officially declared a pandemic—an outbreak that had spread across the world and most people were not immune to it.

Clearly, travel had allowed the virus to spread. Since its initial symptoms were not very different from the common cold, people had not been wary. The air of mystery surrounding the virus didn't help either. As global medical authorities rushed to understand more about COVID-19, one thing was clear—travel had to be restricted, otherwise the spread would become uncontrollable. Terrified countries began limiting international, domestic and even local travel. Educational institutes and offices were closed. Children couldn't go to school. Adults couldn't go to their workplaces. People across the world were urged to remain at home. They were placed under a 'lockdown'.

On 25 March, India imposed a nationwide lockdown with strict travel restrictions. Public transport was curtailed and more than 100 crore people were ordered to stay at home. What unravelled thereafter laid bare the achievements and failures of India's development in the years since Independence.

Where Do the Poor Go?

Economic development has allowed India to generate more employment opportunities, raise incomes and lift crores of people out of destitution. Despite this, not everyone is able to afford a home. This is especially the case in big towns and cities that have more job opportunities and are so overcrowded that it's difficult to find affordable homes. A large number of people living in these areas earn barely enough to rent a roof over their heads and pay for food and other basic requirements. They live in cramped rooms that do not have any toilets or water supply and suffer frequent power cuts. The lockdown not only confined crores of Indians to such dwellings, it also halted economic activity as most workplaces were closed down. Hordes of workers, mainly daily-wage earners and labourers, were suddenly left jobless. This was a huge blow for them. How would they make ends meet in the midst of a lockdown?

Many of them had left their villages to migrate to big towns and cities in search of a livelihood. But with no money coming in, it would be impossible to survive. They had to return home. With public transport curtailed, most of them had only one option left—to ignore the lockdown and either walk or cycle back home. So, even as the world was plagued by sickness and death, the news headlines in India reported one of the greatest mass migrations in history.

Migrant workers from cities walking back to their homes

Highways around the country were besieged by groups of workers and their families. Many of them belonged to relatively underdeveloped states like Uttar Pradesh and Bihar and were returning from cities like Delhi and Mumbai. They had to walk hundreds of kilometres to reach their villages. The journey was tremendously long and difficult. The weather was hot. They had neither enough money nor enough food and water. In some places they got beaten up by the police for violating the lockdown. Many of them died before reaching home—instead of the virus, hardship had claimed their lives.

The government announced a slew of relief measures, offering food and money to aid the poor in the battle against COVID. But it could not reach the migrant workers on time. Transport may have helped, but no one thought of making these arrangements till the plight of the workers was all over the news. Some states began bus services, but these were insufficient. It was not until May that trains were started for workers who were still stranded in places away from home. As early as February, India had flown back citizens who were stranded overseas on special flights. It had a clear record of these stranded persons and planned their evacuation on time. Unfortunately, such records and planning appeared to be missing in the case of workers within the country.

Coordination and coverage are always challenging when such a massive number of people are affected by a sudden calamity. How does a country ensure that relief measures reach everyone on time? Delays and shortfalls are unfortunately inevitable. Yet the desperate spectacle of poverty that played out immediately after the lockdown was announced revealed major shortcomings in the way India's economy has developed.

The Job Problem

Even though job opportunities have increased, they are not evenly distributed. In rural areas, agriculture is usually the biggest employer, but it primarily offers employment during the sowing and harvesting season. The rest of the time, people don't have any steady work. So, they move to urban areas, taking up jobs in factories, offices, etc. Many of them open roadside stalls, selling tea and snacks for instance, or work as plumbers, painters, gardeners, press wallas, barbers, etc. Sometimes, these urban areas are within the same state. But quite often, they are located outside. This is because some states have developed much more than others.

A majority of these workers hold informal jobs. This means that their jobs are not officially recorded. They can be fired any time. Moreover, their employers are not legally bound to provide them good wages, safe working conditions or additional benefits, such as healthcare and accommodation. Unfortunately, the quest for profit has made such jobs far more common than regular and formal employment, which costs more. But most workers are in need of money and lack the education to resist such jobs. It is because of this situation that so many of them ended up jobless during the lockdown. With no economic activity, their employers neither had any need for their services, nor were they responsible for ensuring their well-being. Those who did this did it out of their own goodwill. But a majority didn't. Even the government couldn't help them in a timely and well-planned manner. So, they ended up on the streets, making India intensely aware of their presence and how badly it had failed them.

Healthcare Crisis

Employment opportunities and rising income are certainly an important measure of development. But they are incomplete if they are unable to ensure basic human needs, such as food, clothing, shelter and good health. After all, people usually earn money so they can afford to lead better lives.

Accessible and affordable healthcare that offers relief from sickness is essential to help people lead better lives. A crisis like the pandemic makes the need for such a healthcare system even more urgent. Yet most countries found themselves lacking. Given its large population, the scarcity was especially serious in India.

At the end of April 2021, India became the first country in the world to report four lakh infections in a single day. A new variant of the COVID-19 virus was spreading rapidly across the country, including its rural districts, which had remained largely safe till then. It infected the respiratory system so badly that many patients needed artificial oxygen to breathe. India's healthcare system—hospitals, clinics, doctors, nurses, medical supplies—that had already been stretched, suffered a massive meltdown. Artificial oxygen had to be imported in large quantities from other countries. People were running from pillar to post in search of hospital beds, doctors, nurses and oxygen. Private hospitals and clinics were charging astronomical prices for treatment. Many unscrupulous traders made quick profits, often on fake supplies. Yet, desperate families took whatever they could get. Many patients—especially in underserved rural areas—died because they ran out of breath. Between 1 and 26 May, more than 80 lakh people were infected and over a lakh died. Room for cremating or burying the dead ran out. What transpired in India became a global tragedy that was reported extensively in international media.

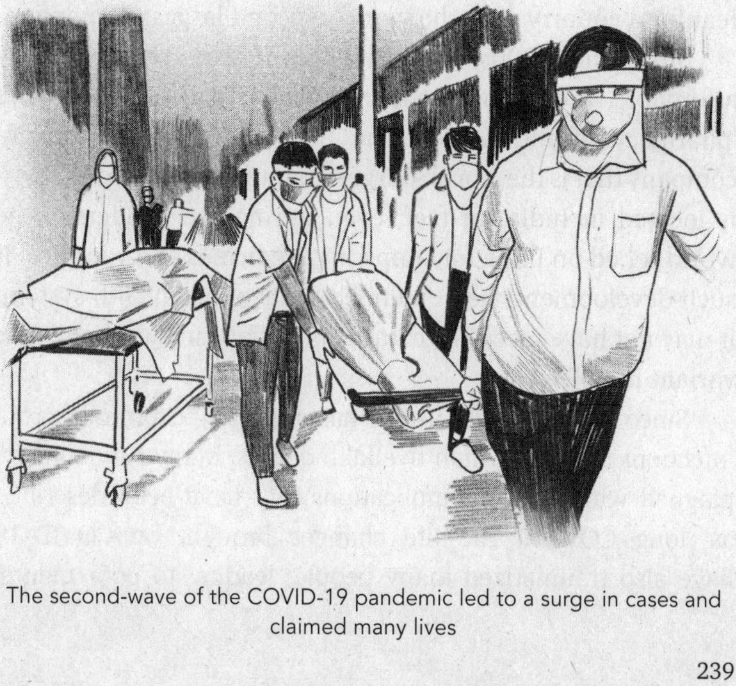

The second-wave of the COVID-19 pandemic led to a surge in cases and claimed many lives

India's poor public health system seems even more ironic when compared to its otherwise impressive medical records. Scientists at the National Institute of Virology were able to gather essential information on COVID-19 within weeks. India developed testing kits in March 2020 and began trials for Covaxin—a locally-developed vaccine—in May. On 16 January 2021, the country began vaccinating its population with Covaxin and Covishield, another vaccine that had been developed in the UK but was being produced in India. In addition to the problems caused by the new variant, India overcame various other challenges to vaccinate its people. Supplying vaccines to the remotest corners of the country was never going to be easy. Basic awareness on hygiene is largely missing and people were unsure about getting vaccinated. Yet, India mounted a successful campaign of awareness, including free and subsidized vaccines. By March 2022, over 80 per cent of its adult population had been vaccinated—a mean feat for a country with the world's second largest population.

Since the 2000s, India has been exporting so many affordable, life-saving medicines that it is often called the 'pharmacy of the world'. The Serum Institute—a private company that is the world's largest manufacturer of vaccines—is located in India. In fact, even during the pandemic, the world relied on India for supplying medicines and vaccines. If such developments had extended to its public health system, it may not have faced the catastrophe that came with the new variant in 2021.

Since March 2020, India has reported over four crore infections and more than five lakh deaths. Many survivors are plagued with health complications that have been described as 'long COVID'. The life changes brought by COVID-19 have also traumatized many people, leading to poor mental health. Scientists have said that pandemics never really end. Eventually, people become immune to the disease either through exposure to the illness or by getting vaccinated against it. What is worrisome is that outbreaks of various infectious diseases, such as SARS, bird flu, Nipah and Zika, have become increasingly common over the past few years. Even though not at all of them may lead to a pandemic, they make it amply clear that India needs to make healthcare an urgent priority and increase and upgrade public health services.

Digital Divide

Over the past few years, India has been focusing heavily on the spread of technology. In July 2015, the government launched the Digital India initiative to empower the country in the field of technology. The initiative seeks to make government services available electronically to citizens by improving online infrastructure and internet connectivity across the country. Since then, the percentage of internet users in India has increased from about 30 per cent to nearly 50 per cent. Yet, crores of Indians continue to lack access to the internet. The pandemic exposed the perils of this digital divide.

In January 2020, the Supreme Court declared that access to the internet was a fundamental right, since it was a source of information for lakhs of citizens. A few days later, India reported its first COVID case and by the end of March, the country was under a strict lockdown. At the time, more than 50 crore Indians were internet users and even more came online in the months thereafter. Confined to their homes, the internet became the only means of connecting to the world outside for many. It allowed them to work from home and entertain themselves. For crores of children, education came home through the internet. But what of those who did not have access to it?

One of the greatest fallouts of the digital divide was on education. Crores of children from poor households lost valuable years of education because they did not have the means to study online. Some belonged to families that did not own any devices, like computers and smartphones, that could be used to connect to the internet. Some families had many people sharing one device and could not spare it all the time for their children's education. Others struggled to cope with the requirements of online classes that needed greater supervision by parents and regular power supply. Without regular schooling, many children, especially girls, belonging to poor families could not continue their studies because they got entangled in housework and helping their parents make a living.

Sustainable Development

Covid-19 is widely believed to be a zoonotic virus—a virus that was transmitted to humans from animals. In fact, most of the recent disease outbreaks have been caused by zoonotic viruses. For example, in 2016, Gujarat reported the first case of the Zika virus that was transmitted from mosquitoes. Similarly, in 2018, Kerala had a Nipah virus outbreak that was traced to fruit bats. The increase in such diseases is often a result of blurring the boundaries between the human and animal world. As human development claims more and more land for itself, room for animals continues to shrink. This increases the contact between humans and animals and makes it easy for viruses to jump to the human species. Although not all viruses are harmful, some of them can cause diseases and sometimes, these diseases can become pandemics. One of the most important lessons of the pandemic has been the need for sustainable development that respects natural resources and does not violate wildlife.

Hope for the Future

India has come a long way since Independence and carved an important place for itself in the world. Yet, the experiences of the pandemic years bear many lessons on development. To become a global superpower, India needs to not only grow its economy but also improve its record in meeting basic human requirements, such as education and healthcare, and find ways of developing without harming the natural world excessively. All this may seem difficult, but it is essential to build a better future.

Most of all, India needs to think about its children, who have possibly suffered the most during the pandemic years. Although COVID-19 has largely spared children, it has taken away a great deal of attention from their needs. Job losses pushed crores of families into poverty. Children in these families lost access to sufficient and nutritious food, and education. Lakhs of children missed routine immunization against diseases like measles and polio because the healthcare system was overwhelmed by the pandemic. The lockdown confined many of them to deeply oppressive home environments where they were deprived of basic needs and even suffered abuse.

The children of today are a mirror to the future. India must look long and hard at them. In the years since Independence, it has produced several miracles in fields like space, technology and medicine. Yet, its greatest miracle may lie in how it saves its children from the darkness of the pandemic years and other perils, and leads them towards a sunlit future.

Keeping Hope Alive

No nation is perfect. It is usually a work in progress. India certainly is. Its progress, especially since the economic changes of 1991, has invited much praise as well as criticism. The pandemic had been one of the greatest challenges to India's progress in the years since Independence. For many people, it has been easy to lose hope in this nation. After all, there are so many things that are wrong with it. The history of Independent India has many accounts of its failures. However, these should not take away from its hard-won successes. While hopelessness might seem easy, the story of this nation has been built on hope—the ability of its greatest leaders and countless people to rise above the problems surrounding them, to persist, protest and prevail.

Decades after Independence: A Timeline

Other timelines: Remaking India's Map (*pages 39-41*), Lok Sabha Elections in India (*pages 65-69*), Major wars fought by Independent India (*page pages 79-80*), India in Space (*pages 107-110*)

1947-1950

- 1947: Independence and Partition
- 1948: Atomic Energy Commission is established, beginning India's quest for atomic power; Independent India wins its first Olympic gold for field hockey; Films Division is founded to promote film production in India; University Education Commission set up to enunciate the goals and objectives of higher education; Cadbury chocolates introduced in India
- 1949: Integration of the states into the Union of India ends with the creation of several administrative units; Constitution of India is adopted
- 1950: First Republic Day

1950-1959

1951: Constitution is amended for the first time—opening the door for various other amendments down the decades; First population census after Independence; First Asian Games are held in Delhi to bring unity among Asian nations; Polling begins in the first elections in Independent India

1952: Athlete K.D. Jadhav becomes the first Indian to win an individual Olympic medal; Secondary Education Commission set up to dwell upon the goals and objectives of secondary education in relation to primary and higher education.

1954: National Film Awards are instituted to honour Indian films. First National Award for the best feature film goes to the Marathi film, *Shyamchi Aai*; Sahitya Akademi is established to promote Indian literature in English and all Indian languages

1956: Reorganization of India's map leads to the creation of 14 states and 6 Union territories, which continue to evolve down the decades

1958: Insurgency in Nagaland (ongoing) that spreads across the north-east in the coming decades; Defence Research and Development Organisation (DRDO) set up to begin military research and development; Bravery awards instituted for children after a fourteen-year-old boy saves Nehru from a fire; Runner Milkha Singh wins India's first gold medal at the Commonwealth Games

1960-1969

- 1961: Non-aligned Movement is founded; National Council of Educational Research and Training (NCERT) set up as an advisory body on school curriculum
- 1962: Indo-China War ends in India's defeat; India launches its space programme
- 1963: Sucheta Kriplani becomes the first woman Chief Minister of a state (Uttar Pradesh)
- 1964: The Bollywood romance *Sangam* becomes the first Indian film to be shot abroad; Kothari Commission set up to study the problems in the education system.
- 1966: Indira Gandhi becomes the first woman prime minister of India, and the second in the world; Reita Faria of India becomes the first Asian woman to win the Miss World beauty pageant
- 1967: Naxalite Movement originates as a peasant movement in Naxalbari, West Bengal; For the first time since Independence, the Congress fairs poorly in elections that see the emergence of powerful regional parties and mark the rise of coalition politics where several parties get together to form a government; Green Revolution transforms Indian agriculture
- 1968: Composer Pandit Ravi Shankar becomes the first Indian to win a Grammy, among the most prestigious awards for music, for the album *West Meets East*; A national policy on education is formulated for the first time, laying the ground for various others in the coming decades.

1970–1979

1970: Operation Flood is launched, transforming India into a leading producer of milk

1974: India tests its first nuclear bomb; Widespread student protests led by JP Narayan rock the government

1975: India put under a state of Emergency

1977: M.G. Ramachandran is the first film actor to become Chief Minister of a state (Tamil Nadu)

1978: First test-tube baby in India and the second worldwide born in Calcutta

1979: C.H. Mohammed Koya becomes the first Indian Union Muslim League member to be sworn in as Chief Minister of a state (Kerala)

1980–1989

1981: Salman Rushdie becomes the first Indian-origin writer to win a Booker Prize, among the most prestigious awards for English literature, for his book *Midnight's Children*. The novel goes on to win the Booker of Bookers in 1993 and the Best of the Booker in 2008, putting the spotlight on Indian literature in English

1982: Colour TV introduced in India

1983: India wins the First Cricket World Cup; Nestle's Maggi noodles introduced in India; Costume designer Bhanu Athaiya becomes the first Indian to win an Academy Award (Oscar), one of the most prestigious awards for films, for her work in Richard Attenborough's *Gandhi*;

India establishes Dakshin Gangotri, its first scientific base station in Antarctica

1984: Bhopal Gas Tragedy draws national attention to industrial safety and environmental concerns; Insurgency in Punjab (ended in the 1990s); *Hum Log* (We the People), India's first drama series in Hindi, begins to air on Doordarshan; Malayalam movie *My Dear Kuttichathan* is the first 3-D film in India; India's first metro railway comes up in Calcutta; Bachendri Pal becomes the first Indian woman to reach the summit of Mount Everest, the tallest mountain in the world

1985: The South Asian Association for Regional Cooperation (SAARC) is founded to promote cooperation among the seven South Asian countries: India, Pakistan, Bangladesh, Bhutan, Nepal, Sri Lanka and Maldives; Indira Gandhi National Open University (IGNOU) becomes the first national university dedicated to distance education

1986: In the aftermath of the Bhopal Gas Tragedy, the government passes the Environmental Protection Act, a landmark legislation to safeguard the natural environment and all living beings from the perils of unsafe industrialization.

1989: Insurgency in Kashmir (ongoing)

1990–1999

1990: Implementation of reservation for Other Backward Castes recommended by the Mandal Commission leads to massive protests

- 1991: Economic reforms transform India; DNA fingerprinting is introduced and begins to be used as evidence in court
- 1992: Demolition of the Babri Masjid sparks off intense communal riots
- 1995: Launch of the internet and mobile phone mark the beginning of a digital revolution in India
- 1998: India declares itself a nuclear-weapon state after testing five nuclear bombs

2000–2009

- 2000: India welcomes its billionth baby; twenty-four-hour news channels introduced in India; Parliament passes the Information Technology Act for electronic, digital and online transactions and cybercrime; Manipuri activist Irom Sharmila begins a historic fast against the Armed Forces Special Powers Act (AFSPA)
- 2001: A major earthquake shakes Gujarat on Republic Day; Narendra Modi becomes the Chief Minister of Gujarat and goes on to become the Prime Minister of India in 2014
- 2004: An undersea earthquake near Sumatra leads to a tsunami that wreaks havoc in several places around the world, including coastal Tamil Nadu
- 2005: Parliament passes the Right to Information Act that allows citizens to ask for information from any government authority; Google's Orkut marks the advent of social media in India. Facebook follows in 2006.

2007: In the aftermath of the tsunami, India launches an early warning system that helps to save many lives by giving advance warnings of natural disasters along India's vast coastline; Pratibha Patil becomes the first woman President of India

2008: Terrorists storm various locations in Mumbai, killing hundreds of people; India announces National Action Plan for Climate Change; Tata launches Nano, claimed to be the world's cheapest car; Sister Alphonsa Muttathupadathu becomes the first woman of Indian-origin to be canonized by the Roman Catholic Church; Danny Boyle's *Slumdog Millionaire*, a British film based on Vikas Swarup's novel *Q&A*, and set in Dharavi, believed to be the largest slum in Asia, wins eight Oscars; Indian Premier League (IPL), a professional cricket league with twenty-over (T20) matches and teams representing various Indian cities, is established

2009: Sachin Tendulkar becomes the first cricketer to score 30,000 international runs; Parliament passes the Right of Children, in the age group of six to fourteen years, to Free and Compulsory Education (RTE) Act

2010–2019

2011: Anti-corruption agitation led by activist Anna Hazare shakes the government. It leads to the emergence of the Aam Aadmi Party that goes on to score a spectacular victory in the assembly elections in Delhi in 2015

2013: Golden Quadrilateral, a network of highways connecting India's top four metro cities—Delhi, Mumbai, Chennai and Kolkata—is finally completed, giving a major boost to road transport in the country.

- 2015: Reopening of the National Register of Citizens in Assam followed by amendments to the Citizenship Act in 2019 lead to widespread protests
- 2016: All 500- and 1000-rupee notes are withdrawn from circulation, wiping out over 80 per cent of India's currency overnight. New 500- and 2000-rupee notes are issued.
- 2019: The visa-free Kartarpur Corridor, often called the 'Road to Peace', is inaugurated. It links Dera Baba Nanak in Gurdaspur, India to Gurudwara Darbar Sahib, the final resting place of Guru Nanak in Kartarpur, Pakistan.

2020 and beyond

- 2020: India put under a strict lockdown, restricting one-sixth of humanity to home
- 2021: Massive agitation by farmers on the borders of the national capital compels the government to withdraw three new agricultural laws it had proposed
- 2022: *Tomb of Sand*, the English translation of Geetanjali Shree's Hindi novel *Ret Samadhi*, becomes the first translation from an Indian language to win a Booker

Selected Bibliography

Prologue: Freedom at Last

1. Sen Gupta, Subhadra. *The Constitution of India for Children*. Gurugram: Penguin Random House India, 2020
2. Spear, Percival. *The History of India: Volume Two*. New Delhi: Penguin Books, 1998
3. Guha, Ramachandra. *India After Gandhi: The History of the World's Largest Democracy*. London: Pan Macmillan, 2007
4. Dalal, Roshen. *The Puffin History of India Vol. 2*. Gurugram: Penguin Random House India, 2014

Chapter 1: A Divided Land, a Broken Home

1. Spear, Percival. *The History of India: Volume Two*. New Delhi: Penguin Books, 1998
2. Guha, Ramachandra. *India After Gandhi: The History of the World's Largest Democracy*. London: Pan Macmillan, 2007
3. Dalal, Roshen. *The Puffin History of India Vol. 2*. Gurugram: Penguin Random House India, 2014

Chapter 2: Refugee Crisis

1. Guha, Ramachandra. *India After Gandhi: The History of the World's Largest Democracy*. London: Pan Macmillan, 2007

2. Dalal, Roshen. *The Puffin History of India Vol. 2*. Gurgaon: Penguin Random House India, 2014
3. Luthra, P.N. 'Problem of Refugees from East Bengal' *Economic and Political Weekly* Vol. 6, No. 50 (11 December 1971)
4. Tripathi, Sanjeev. 'Illegal Immigration From Bangladesh to India: Toward a Comprehensive Solution' published on carnegieindia.org, 29 June 2016. Retrieved from https://carnegieindia.org/2016/06/29/illegal-immigration-from-bangladesh-to-india-toward-comprehensive-solution-pub-63931
5. Chakravarty, Ipsita. 'On the fence: Fluid and ever changing, the Indo-Bangladesh border defies the idea of a neat boundary' published on *Scroll.in*, 20 January 2018. Retrieved from https://scroll.in/article/865586/on-the-fence-fluid-and-ever-changing-the-indo-bangladesh-border-defies-the-idea-of-a-neat-boundary
6. Shashikumar, VK. 'The Subverted Indo-Bangladesh Border'. *India Defence Review*. Issue Vol 24, 2 Apr-Jun, 2009. Retrieved from http://www.indiandefencereview.com/news/the-subverted-indo-bangladesh-border-i/
7. Goswami, Uddipana. 'Internal Displacement, Migration, and Policy in Northeastern India'. East-West Center Washington Working Papers. No. 8, April 2007. Retrieved from https://www.eastwestcenter.org/sites/default/files/private/EWCW wp008.pdf
8. Chamuah, Parag. 'A brief history of Assam, Assam Movement & Assam Accord and the implementation of NRC & CAA'. *North East Today*, December 23, 2019
9. Assam Public Works Vs Union of India, retrieved from https://indiankanoon.org/doc/135202420/
10. Dutta, Prabash K. 'What is Assam Accord of 1985 and how amended citizenship law challenges it?' *India Today*, 13 December 2019. Retrieved from https://www.indiatoday.in/news-analysis/story/what-is-assam-accord-of-1985-and-how-amended-citizenship-law-challenges-it-1627965-2019-12-13
11. Natarajan, Aruna. 'Explained: Should you read the CAA in conjunction with the proposed NRC?' published on

citizenmatters.in, 17 December 2019. Retrieved from https://citizenmatters.in/faq-on-citizenship-amendment-act-and-nrc-connection-14928

12. Subramanian, Nirupama. 'Explained: On "refugees" and "illegal immigrants", how India's stance changes with circumstances'. *Indian Express*, 13 April 2021. Retrieved from https://indianexpress.com/article/explained/on-refugees-and-illegal-immigrants-how-indias-stance-changes-with-circumstances-7270883/
13. Pooja. 'India's Refugee Policy' published on www.indianbarassociation.org. Retrieved from https://www.indianbarassociation.org/indias-refugee-policy/
14. Tripathi, Rahul. 'Tibetan refugees down from 1.5 lakh to 85,000 in 7 years'. *Indian Express*. 11 September 2018. Retrieved from https://indianexpress.com/article/india/tibetan-refugees-down-from-1-5-lakh-to-85000-in-7-years-5349587/
15. 'Myanmar Rohingya: What you need to know about the crisis', published on bbc.com, 23 January 2020. Retrieved from https://www.bbc.com/news/world-asia-41566561
16. *Rohingyas in India: State of Rohingya Muslims in India in absence of Refugee Law*. The Netherland: Foundation London Story. Retrieved from https://www.ohchr.org/sites/default/files/Documents/Issues/Religion/Islamophobia-AntiMuslim/Civil%20Society%20or%20Individuals/RitumbraM1.pdf
17. Chakravarty, Ipsita. '50 years on, Chakma refugees from Bangladesh are still denied citizenship rights in Arunachal', published online at Scroll.in, 30 July 2017. Retrieved from https://scroll.in/article/845129/50-years-on-chakma-refugees-from-bangladesh-are-still-denied-citizenship-rights-in-arunachal
18. Patel, Mira. 'A history of Sri Lankan refugees in India'. *Indian Express*, 9 April 2022. Retrieved from https://indianexpress.com/article/research/a-history-of-sri-lankan-refugees-in-india-7858886/
19. Thapar Romila, Ram N., Bhatia Gautam and Patel Gautam. *On Citizenship*. New Delhi: Aleph Book Company, 2021
20. Inputs from Raj Sethi

Chapter 3: Remaking the Map

1. Guha, Ramachandra. *India After Gandhi: The History of the World's Largest Democracy*. London: Pan Macmillan, 2007
2. Dalal, Roshen. *A Puffin History of India Vol. 2*. Gurugram: Penguin Random House India, 2014
3. Menon, V.P. *Integration Of The Indian States*. Hyderabad: Orient Blackswan Pvt Ltd, 2011
4. Spear, Percival. *The History of India: Volume Two*. New Delhi: Penguin Books, 1998
5. Dalal, Roshen. *India at 70: Snapshots since Independence*. Gurugram: Penguin Random House India, 2017
6. State Formation in India. Retrieved from https://www.mapsofindia.com/maps/india/formation-of-states.html
7. Ministry of Home Affairs. 'Maps of newly formed Union Territories of Jammu Kashmir and Ladakh, with the map of India'. Press Information Bureau. 2 November 2019. Retrieved from https://pib.gov.in/PressReleasePage.aspx?PRID=1590112

Chapter 4: Ideas of India

1. Guha, Ramachandra. *India After Gandhi: The History of the World's Largest Democracy*. London: Pan Macmillan, 2007
2. Sen Gupta, Subhadra. *The Constitution of India for Children*. Gurugram: Penguin Random House India, 2020
3. Dalal, Roshen. *A Puffin History of India Vol. 2*. Gurugram: Penguin Random House India, 2014
4. Austin, Granville. *The Indian Constitution: Cornerstone of A Nation*. London: Oxford University Press, 1966
5. Constitutional debates. Retrieved from http://164.100.47.194/Loksabhahindi/cadebatefiles/cadebates.html
6. Darbhamulla, Sruthi. 'Explained: The anti-Hindi imposition movements in India'. *The Hindu*, 23 April 2022.
7. Singh, Tripurdaman. *Sixteen Stormy Days: The Story of the First Amendment to the Constitution of India*. Gurugram: Penguin Random House India, 2021

Chapter 5: The Greatest Experiment in Democracy

1. Guha, Ramachandra. *India After Gandhi: The History of the World's Largest Democracy*. London: Pan Macmillan, 2007
2. Election Commission India. Report on the First General Elections in India (1951-52), Volume I (General) New Delhi: Government of India Press, 1955
3. Sen Gupta, Subhadra. *The Constitution of India for Children*. Gurugram: Penguin Random House India, 2020
4. Dalal, Roshen. *A Puffin History of India Vol. 2*. Gurugram: Penguin Random House India, 2014
5. Venkatesh, Karthik. 'India's First Elections: Finally, the Nation Speaks', published on livehistoryindia.com, 24 January 2020. Retrieved from https://www.livehistoryindia.com/story/eras/indias-first-elections-finally-india-speaks

Chapter 6: A Taste of Defeat

1. Guha, Ramachandra. *India After Gandhi: The History of the World's Largest Democracy*. London: Pan Macmillan, 2007
2. Dalal, Roshen. *A Puffin History of India Vol. 2*. Gurugram: Penguin Random House India, 2014
3. Dalvi, J.P. *Himalayan Blunder: The Curtain-Raiser to the Sino-Indian War of 1962*. Delhi: Natraj Publishers (originally published by Thacker and Company Ltd), 1969
4. Singh, Sushant. 'Line of Actual Control (LAC): Where it is located, and where India and China differ' *Indian Express*, 1 June 2020. Retrieved from https://indianexpress.com/article/explained/line-of-actual-control-where-it-is-located-and-where-india-and-china-differ-6436436/
5. Gokhale, Vijay. 'The Road from Galwan: The Future of India-China Relations', published on carnegieindia.org, 10 March 2021. Retrieved from https://carnegieindia.org/2021/03/10/road-from-galwan-future-of-india-china-relations-pub-84019
6. Ministry of External Affairs, 'India-China Bilateral Relations'. Retrieved from https://mea.gov.in/Portal/ForeignRelation/China_October_2017.pdf

7. Banerjee, Avijit. 'India-China Diplomatic Relations: A Perspective', 20 October 2021. Retrieved from https://www.mfa.gov.cn/ce/cgkolkata/eng/zlgxw/t1915624.htm
8. Subramanian, Nirupama. 'Explained: Two years after Galwan clash, where India-China relations stand today' *Indian Express*, 17 June 2022
9. Inputs from Colonel (Retd) Azad Krishna Chaturvedi

Chapter 7: Nuclear Age

1. Perkovich, George. *India's Nuclear Bomb: The Impact on Global Proliferation*. University of California Press, 1999
2. Gupta, Meghaa. *Unearthed: An Environmental History of Independent India*. Gurugram: Penguin Random House India, 2020
3. Guha, Ramachandra. *India After Gandhi: The History of the World's Largest Democracy*. London: Pan Macmillan, 2007

Chapter 8: Rocketing into Space

1. Singh, Gurbir. *The Indian Space Programme: India's Incredible Journey from the Third World to the First*. Astrotalkuk Publications, 2017
2. Indian Space Research Organisation. *From Fishing Hamlet to Red Planet: India's Space Journey*. Edited by Rao, Manoranajan, Suresh B.N. and Balagangadharan, V.P. Noida: Harper Collins India, 2015
3. Sukumar, Arun Mohan. *Midnight's Machines—A Political History of Technology in India*. Gurugram: Penguin Random House India, 2019
4. ISRO's Timeline from 1960s to Today, Retrieved from https://www.isro.gov.in/about-isro/isros-timeline-1960s-to-today

Chapter 9: Fighting Hunger

1. Siegel, Robert Benjamin. *Hungry Nation: Food, Famine and the Making of Modern India*. Cambridge University Press, 2018

2. Guha, Ramachandra. *India After Gandhi: The History of the World's Largest Democracy*. London: Pan Macmillan, 2007
3. Agricultural Development in India. Retrieved from https://www.eklavya.in/pdfs/Books/SSTP/social_studies_8/civics/Agricultural%20Development%20I.pdf
4. Deshpande, R.S. 'Current Land Policy Issues in India' Retrieved from https://www.fao.org/3/y5026e/y5026e0b.htm
5. Sen, Amartya. *The Country of First Boys*. Edited by Sen Antara Dev and Kanjilal Pratik. New Delhi: Oxford University Press, 2015
6. Gupta, Meghaa. *Unearthed: An Environmental History of Independent India*. Gurugram: Penguin Random House India, 2020

Chapter 10: A Billion-Litre Idea

1. Chowdhury, Rohini. *Verghese Kurien: The Milkman of India*. Gurugram: Scholastic India Pvt Ltd, 2014
2. Gupta, Meghaa. *Unearthed: An Environmental History of Independent India*. Gurugram: Penguin Random House India, 2020
3. Kurien, Verghese. 'India's Milk Revolution: Investing in Rural Producer Organizations' from *Ending Poverty in South Asia: Ideas that Work*. Edited by Narayan, Deepa and Glinskaya, Elena. Washington DC: The World Bank, 2007
4. Guha, Ramachandra. *India After Gandhi: The History of the World's Largest Democracy*. London: Pan Macmillan, 2007

Chapter 11: An Era of Protests

1. Guha, Ramachandra. *India After Gandhi: The History of the World's Largest Democracy*. London: Pan Macmillan, 2007
2. Pawar, J.V. *Dalit Panthers: An Authoritative History* (Translated from Marathi by Sonawane, Rakshit). New Delhi: Forward Press Books, 2017
3. Pien, Diane. 'Dalit Panther Movement (1972-1977)' published on blackpast.org, 17 August 2018. Retrieved from https://

www.blackpast.org/global-african-history/dalit-panther-movement-1972-1977/
4. *Cruelty* by Namdeo Dhasal, retrieved from https://www.poemhunter.com/poem/cruelty-27/
5. Maanvi. 'An Angry Nation Reclaims the Screen: Films India Loved in 1970s' published on thequint.com, 14 August 2016. Retrieved from https://www.thequint.com/entertainment/as-she-turns-69-films-which-defined-india-the-angry-70s-amitabh-bcahchan-shahsi-kapoor-sholay-aandhi-bobby#read-more
6. Venkateswaran, Vikram. 'George Reddy to JP: How Student Protests in the 70s Shook Up India', published on thequint.com, 21 December 2019. Retrieved from https://www.thequint.com/explainers/caa-protests-jp-movement-how-students-changed-protests-in-the-70s-jayaprakash-narayanan#read-more
7. Dalal, Roshen. *A Puffin History of India Vol. 2*. Gurugram: Penguin Random House India, 2014

Chapter 12: It's an Emergency

1. Guha, Ramachandra. *India After Gandhi: The History of the World's Largest Democracy*. London: Pan Macmillan, 2007
2. Dalal, Roshen. *A Puffin History of India Vol. 2*. Gurugram: Penguin Random House India, 2014
3. Ministry of External Affairs. Part XVIII: Emergency Provisions. Retrieved from https://www.mea.gov.in/Images/pdf1/Part18.pdf
4. Inputs from Laila Tyabji

Chapter 13: Battling Disunity

1. Guha, Ramachandra. *India After Gandhi: The History of the World's Largest Democracy*. London: Pan Macmillan, 2007
2. Ministry of Home Affairs. The Armed Forces (Special Forces) Act, 1958. Retrieved from https://www.mha.gov.in/sites/default/files/armed_forces_special_powers_act1958.pdf

3. Amnesty International. 'India: Briefing on the Armed Forces (Special Powers) Act, 1958'. Retrieved from https://www.amnesty.org/en/wp-content/uploads/2021/08/asa200252005en.pdf
4. Safi, Michael. 'How love and a taste of honey bought one Indian woman's 16-year hunger strike to an end'. *The Guardian*. 11 November 2018. Retrieved from https://www.theguardian.com/world/2018/nov/11/irom-sharmila-love-story-worlds-longest-hunger-strike
5. Goswami, Uddipana. 'Internal Displacement, Migration, and Policy in Northeastern India'. East-West Center Washington Working Papers. No. 8, April 2007. Retrieved from https://www.eastwestcenter.org/sites/default/files/private/EWCWwp008.pdf
6. Bhaumik, Subir. 'Insurgencies in India's Northeast: Conflict, Co-option & Change'. East-West Center Washington Working Papers. No. 10, July 2007. Retrieved from https://scholarspace.manoa.hawaii.edu/server/api/core/bitstreams/45471990-933f-4ea7-99fe-02c9e7e4b9ff/content
7. Press Trust of India. 'AFSPA now applicable fully only in 31 districts of 4 Northeast states'. *Business Standard*, 1 April 2022
8. Karmakar, Rahul. 'AFSPA should go entirely because of the impunity it offers armed forces'. *The Hindu*, 2 May 2022
9. Karmakar, Rahul. 'Centre keen on lifting AFSPA from northeast: PM Modi'. *The Hindu*, 28 April 2022.
10. Sekhon, Jagrup Singh and Singh, Nirmal. 'Rise, Dynamics, and Decline of Violence in Punjab: A Critical Reassessment of Existing Explanations'. Retrieved from https://punjab.global.ucsb.edu/sites/default/files/sitefiles/4-Sekhon%20%26%20Singh%20FINAL%2022.1.pdf
11. Telford, Hamish. 'Counter-Insurgency in India: Observations from Punjab and Kashmir'. *Journal of Conflict Studies*, 21(1). Retrieved from https://journals.lib.unb.ca/index.php/JCS/article/view/4293
12. Inputs from Dr S.K. Gupta

Chapter 14: The World's Worst Industrial Disaster

1. Mahapatra Richard, Yadav Archana, Bhushan Chandra, Varshney Vibha, Narain Sunita, Sharma Aruna, Gupta Kaushik. *Bhopal Gas Tragedy After 30 years*. New Delhi: Centre for Science and Environment, 2014
2. Union Carbide Corporation vs Union Of India Etc. Retrieved from https://indiankanoon.org/doc/1344892/
3. Gupta, Meghaa. *Unearthed: An Environmental History of Independent India*. Gurugram: Penguin Random House India,2020

Chapter 15: Where's the Money?

1. Pai, Roopa. *So You Want to Know About Economics*. New Delhi: Rupa Publications Pvt Ltd, 2017
2. Panagariya, Arvind. *India: The Emerging Giant*. New York: Oxford University Press, 2008.
3. Guha, Ramachandra. *India After Gandhi: The History of the World's Largest Democracy*. London: Pan Macmillan, 2007
4. Adhia, Nimish. 'The History of India's Economic Development since Independence'. *Education About Asia*. Volume 20:3 (Winter 2015): India: Past, Present, and Future. Retrieved from https://www.asianstudies.org/publications/eaa/archives/the-history-of-economic-development-in-india-since-independence/
5. Budget Speech of Shri Manmohan Singh, Minister of Finance (24 July 1991). Retrieved from https://www.indiabudget.gov.in/budget2021-22/doc/bspeech/bs199192.pdf
6. Sen, Amartya. *The Country of First Boys*. Edited by Sen Antara Dev and Kanjilal Pratik. New Delhi: Oxford University Press, 2015
7. Inputs from K.R. Prithviraj

Chapter 16: Technology Comes Home

1. Sukumar, Arun Mohan. *Midnight's Machines—A Political History of Technology in India*. Gurugram: Penguin Random House India, 2019

2. Arnold, David. *Everyday Technology: Machines and the Making of India's Modernity*. The University of Chicago Press, 2013
3. Development of Radio, retrieved from https://www.shcollege.ac.in/wp-content/uploads/NAAC_Documents_IV_Cycle/Criterion-II/2.3.2/DevelopmentofRadio.pdf
4. Archana, KC. '80 years of AIR: Remembering the golden days of All India Radio'. *India Today*. 8 June 2016. Retrieved from https://www.indiatoday.in/fyi/story/80-years-of-air-remembering-the-golden-days-of-all-india-radio-12987-2016-06-08
5. Iyengar, Radhika. 'In 1952, Hindi film songs were banned on All India Radio'. *Mint*. 13 July 2018. Retrieved from https://www.livemint.com/Leisure/XUjIcb1XdO60gXOrHCyH2H/In-1952-Hindi-film-songs-were-banned-on-All-India-Radio.html
6. Pothukuchi, Madhavi. 'Iconic Akashvani tune to secret station and banned songs—India's tryst with radio waves'. *The Print*. 13 February, 2020. Retrieved from https://theprint.in/features/iconic-akashvani-tune-to-secret-station-and-banned-songs-indias-tryst-with-radio-waves/364501/
7. Sheopurkar, Shruti & Srinivasan, Nalini. 'Community Radio—Its Evolution and Effectiveness in Rural Development' Bharat Inclusion Initiative. 12 February 2021. Retrieved from https://medium.com/bharatinclusion/community-radio-its-evolution-and-effectiveness-in-rural-development-3efa3cace74e
8. *Community Radio in South Asia: Reclaiming the Airwaves.* Edited by Malik, Kanchan K and Pavarala, Vinod. Routledge, 2020.
9. Anna FM, Retrieved from https://www.annauniv.edu/MediaScience/AnnaFM.php
10. Mehta, Nalin. 'Indian Media at Seventy: Five Big Challenges' from *Seven Decades of Independent India Ideas and Reflections*. Edited by Rai, Vinod and Palit, Dr Amitendu. New Delhi: Penguin Random House India, 2018
11. Guha, Ramachandra. *India After Gandhi: The History of the World's Largest Democracy*. London: Pan Macmillan, 2007

12. Sharma, Dinesh C. *The Outsourcer: The Story of India's IT Revolution*. Massachusetts Institute of Technology (originally published by Harper Collins India), 2015
13. 'Y2K Bug'. Retrieved from https://education.nationalgeographic.org/resource/Y2K-bug
14. Agrawal, Ravi. *India Connected: How the Smartphone is Transforming the World's Largest Democracy*. New York: Oxford University Press, 2018
15. Gupta, Meghaa. *Unearthed: An Environmental History of Independent India*. Gurugram: Penguin Random House India, 2020
16. Press Trust of India. 'History made: mobiles outpace landline' *Economic Times*, 30 December 2004. Retrieved from https://economictimes.indiatimes.com/log-out-04-log-in-05/history-made-mobiles-outpace-landline/articleshow/975754.cms?from=mdr
17. *Internet Adoption in India.* Report by Internet and Mobile Association of India (IAMAI) and Kantar, June 2021. Retrieved from https://images.assettype.com/afaqs/2021-06/b9a3220f-ae2f-43db-a0b4-36a372b243c4/KANTAR_ICUBE_2020_Report_C1.pdf
18. Inputs by Karan Mahajan and Vimla

Chapter 18: One Nation, Many Religions

1. Guha, Ramachandra. *India After Gandhi: The History of the World's Largest Democracy*. London: Pan Macmillan, 2007
2. 'Triple talaq: India criminalises Muslim 'instant divorce' published on bbc.com, 30 July 2019. Retrieved from https://www.bbc.com/news/world-asia-india-49160818
3. Rao, Jayesh. 'Implementation Of Uniform Civil Code In India' Retrieved from https://www.legalserviceindia.com/legal/article-4743-implementation-of-uniform-civil-code-in-india.html
4. Biswas, Soutik. 'UCC: The coming storm over a single common law in India' published on bbc.com, 30 May 2019. Retrieved from https://www.bbc.com/news/world-asia-india-61589491

5. Dalal, Roshen. *A Puffin History of India Vol. 2*. Gurugram: Penguin Random House India, 2014
6. 'Ayodhya Verdict: Full Text'. Retrieved from https://indianexpress.com/article/india/ayodhya-verdict-full-text-supreme-court-6111349/
7. Essa, Azad. 'Kashmiri Pandits: Why we never fled Kashmir' published on www.aljazeera.com, 2 August 2011. Retrieved from https://www.aljazeera.com/news/2011/8/2/kashmiri-pandits-why-we-never-fled-kashmir
8. Subramanian, Nirupama. 'Explained: The Kashmir Pandit tragedy'. *Indian Express*. 24 January 2020. Retrieved from https://indianexpress.com/article/explained/exodus-of-kashmiri-pandits-from-valley-6232410/
9. Kaul, Ashok. "My last wish': A Kashmiri Pandit's Letter To Muslim Friend Back Home After 1990 Exodus' published on www.outlookindia.com, 24 April 2022. Retrieved from https://www.outlookindia.com/culture-society/my-last-wish-a-kashmiri-pandit-letter-to-muslim-friend-back-home-after-1990-exodus-news-192983
10. Jaffrelot, Christophe. 'The Fate of Secularism in India' from *The BJP in Power: Indian Democracy and Religious Nationalism*. Edited by Vaishnav, Milan. Carnegie Endowment for International Peace, 2019. Retrieved from https://carnegieendowment.org/2019/04/04/fate-of-secularism-in-india-pub-78689
11. Inputs from Safina Nabi

Chapter 19: Electrified!

1. Kale, Sunila S. *Electrifying India: Regional Political Economies of Development*. Stanford University Press, 2014
2. Nhalur Sreekumar, Chitnis Ashwini, Vaishnava Saumya, Gambhir Ashwin. *Know Your Power* (3rd Revised Edition). Pune: Prayas (Energy Group), 2019
3. Vasudevan Reshmi, Cherail Koshy, Bhatia Ramesh and Jayaram Nisha. *Energy Efficiency in India: History and Overview*. New Delhi: Alliance for an Energy Efficient Economy, 2011

4. Ministry of Statistics and Programme Implementation (2022). *Energy Statistics*. Retrieved from https://mospi.gov.in/documents/213904/1606151/Energy%20Statistics%20India%202022164482594802.pdf/aed59aac-4d5a-995b-1232-bb68397cd873
5. Agrawal Shalu, Mani Sunil, Jain Abhishek, Ganesan Karthik. *State of Electricity Access in India*. New Delhi: Council on Energy, Environment and Water, 2020
6. Ritchie Hannah, Roser Max, Rosado Pablo. 'CO_2 and Greenhouse Gas Emissions'. 2020. Published online at OurWorldInData.org. Retrieved from https://ourworldindata.org/co2/country/india#citation

Epilogue: Pandemic Years and Beyond

1. 'The Whistleblower who succumbed to COVID-19', 'Twice Bitten', 'Unprepared Still', 'This is Why', 'Residual Pandemic', 'Fault Lines', 'Forced Migration', 'A Generation Interrupted', 'Edge of Crisis', 'Socio-economic Shifts Likely in Future', 'Long-term Impacts Warrant Concern', 'Focus on Mental Health', 'Troubled Interiors' from *Down To Earth* (1-15 January 2022) Vol 30, No 16
2. Salve, Prachi. '90% Of Jobs Created Over Two Decades Post-Liberalisation Were Informal' published online at www.indiaspend.com, 9 May 2019. Retrieved from https://www.indiaspend.com/90-of-jobs-created-over-two-decades-post-liberalisation-were-informal/
3. Srija A and Shirke Shrinivas V. *An Analysis of the Informal Labour Market in India*. Confederation of Indian Industry, 2014. Retrieved from https://www.ies.gov.in/pdfs/CII%20EM-october-2014.pdf
4. Patel, Dr Champa. 'COVID-19: The Hidden Majority in India's Migration Crisis' published online at www.chathamhouse.org, 13 July 2020. Retrieved from https://1/2020/07/covid-19-hidden-majority-indias-migration-crisis
5. Seervai Shanoor and Shah Arnav. 'India's Failure of Leadership Collapses Health System in COVID-19 Surge' published on

www.commonwealthfund.org, 29 April 2021. Retrieved from https://www.commonwealthfund.org/blog/2021/indias-failure-leadership-collapses-health-system-covid-19-surge

6. Dey, Sushmi. '80% of India's adults now fully vaccinated, 97% got 1st shot: Government', 20 February, 2022. Retrieved from https://timesofindia.indiatimes.com/india/80-of-indias-adults-now-fully-vaccinated-97-got-1st-shot-government/articleshow/89696050.cms
7. Masurkar, Nikkhil S. 'Why is India the Pharmacy of the World?' *Financial Express*, 25 September 2021. Retrieved from https://www.financialexpress.com/lifestyle/health/why-is-india-the-pharmacy-of-the-world/2337554/
8. Krishnan, Revathi. 'More people in India got internet access in 2020, but fewer mobile connections: Niti report' published online at theprint.in, 10 June 2021. Retrieved from https://theprint.in/india/more-people-in-india-got-internet-access-in-2020-but-fewer-mobile-connections-niti-report/675324/
9. Dutta, Prabash K. 'Internet access a fundamental right, Supreme Court makes it official: Article 19 explained' *India Today*, 10 January 2020. Retrieved from https://www.indiatoday.in/news-analysis/story/internet-access-fundamental-right-supreme-court-makes-official-article-19-explained-1635662-2020-01-10
10. Modi Sushma and Postaria Ronika. 'How COVID-19 deepens the digital education divide in India' published on www.weforum.org, 5 October 2020. Retrieved from https://www.weforum.org/agenda/2020/10/how-covid-19-deepens-the-digital-education-divide-in-india/
11. Sen, Amartya. *The Country of First Boys*. Edited by Sen Antara Dev and Kanjilal Pratik. New Delhi: Oxford University Press, 2015

Acknowledgements

To historians whose books have offered me a rich education on the multifaceted narratives of modern India, especially Ramachandra Guha. Reading his phenomenal *India After Gandhi* got me hooked to contemporary history and convinced me that we needed such texts for young readers to help them make sense of the times. I must also thank him for the uncommon courtesy of replying to most of the emails I have badgered him with, over the years.

Sohini Mitra, who prodded me to keep writing books. Her unwavering support has seen me through many dark days of self-doubt during my nascent writing journey.

Smit Zaveri, an editor who always makes me think harder about my work.

Sayan Mukherjee, for pulling off a miracle with the artworks in record-time.

Shalini Agrawal, Samar Bansal, Prerna Chatterjee and the team at Penguin Random House India for bringing this book to life—may it be long and fruitful.

Arvind Sardana, for vetting the narratives in this book and the deeply educative conversations that helped me fine-tune them.

Romila Thapar, O.P. Agarwal, Manasa Gade, Sreekumar Nhalur and Rubin D'Cruz for reviewing various chapters. Their thoughtful suggestions have added immensely to the narrative.

Manu S. Pillai for being a kind and sincere foreword-writer.

Disha Shetty and Tripurdaman Singh for their generous endorsements.

Raj Sethi, Colonel (retd) Azad Krishna Chaturvedi, Rajiv Gupta, Laila Tyabji, Dr S.K. Gupta, K.R. Prithviraj, Karan Mahajan, Vimla, Safina Nabi and Shanta Bijawat for sharing their stories with me and allowing me to put them in this book. I am truly grateful.

Radhika Menon, most of what I know about a good children's book is because of my years working with Tulika Publishers.

Friends, readers and well-wishers, who have kept me going through some very trying times with their unstinting support.

The team at GLF/SN for giving me space and time on hectic days, and never complaining.

Most of all, to my family—mom, dad and bhai—for always having my back, sharing my joys, seeing me through my tears and making life meaningful every single day. I'm here because of you.